SPENDING, FAST AND SLOW

$PENDING FAST AND SLOW

Why your money disappears so fast and how to slow down the flow

MAX PHELPS

MACMILLAN

First published in 2024 by Major Street Publishing Pty Ltd

First published in India 2024 by Macmillan
an imprint of Pan Macmillan Publishing India Private Limited
707 Kailash Building
26 K. G. Marg, New Delhi 110001
www.panmacmillan.co.in

Pan Macmillan, The Smithson, 6 Briset Street, Farringdon, London EC1M 5NR
Associated companies throughout the world
www.panmacmillan.com

ISBN 978-93-6113-127-1

1 3 5 7 9 8 6 4 2

Internal design by Production Works
Printed and bound in India by Gopsons Papers Pvt. Ltd., Noida

Contents

Contents

Introduction

In today's world, it's all too easy to find ourselves swept away by consumerism, instant gratification and debt – or just feel as if we're not getting ahead as fast as we should be. Money, like sand, seems to slip through our fingers, leaving us wondering where it all went and how we can regain control. We're also facing rising housing costs, whether we're renters or mortgage holders, and inflation is pushing up the cost of everything else.

If you pay attention to most financial commentators in the media, you could be forgiven for thinking that you're the problem and you need to change your attitude to money. I've been married for 31 years and long ago realised that my wife, Kelly, is completely different to me with money and can't just change.

The obvious solution to money woes – the rational solution, even – is to spend less and save more, cut out unnecessary purchases and spend only on what's strictly necessary after searching out the best value. However, in my experience, only 10% of people behave rationally with money all day every day – and this minority is normally referred to as 'Scrooges', 'tight-arses', 'accountants' or 'financial planners'. The other 90% of us – including the partners of this minority group, like Kelly – behave normally. They want stuff, they seem to have enough money, and the maths is too hard and too boring for them to calculate the consequences of every decision they make.

So, where does that leave people who are struggling to get ahead, who find they're consistently missing their saving goals or whose credit card debt just isn't shrinking, despite their best efforts?

I don't believe that the solution is depriving yourself of life's pleasures or forcing yourself into a miserly existence. Instead, it's about understanding the deep-rooted psychological factors that drive your spending habits and learning how to harness them to create a life of financial stability and true abundance. By slowing down your spending and setting up structures that trigger you to think before you spend, you can make better decisions every day – and ultimately get more out of life.

In the chapters to come, I'll delve into the fascinating intersection of psychology and money, exploring how our brains are wired to approach financial decisions large and small, and provide strategies to make it harder to spend thoughtlessly to help you stay on track.

Thinking – and spending – in the real world

I've long been fascinated by people's behaviour with money and why what they think they do and what they actually do are so different. Let me illustrate by sharing a conversation I had with a young couple recently:

Me:	How much do you spend each month?
Daniel:	Around $2000.
Me:	That seems really low! The average is $3000 a month. How much is your credit card bill?
Susan:	Around $4000.
Me:	…

This is typical of hundreds of conversations that I've had as a finance professional over the past decade and a half. Daniel and Susan believed they were spending $1000 a month less than the average, when in fact they were spending $1000 *more* than the average and $2000 more than they first thought.

This pattern of thought isn't unique to month-to-month spending practices, either. One study suggests that people underestimate future spending by 27%. In fact, my wife and I had this problem for over a decade before discovering, by sheer luck, a better way to manage our money.

When I became a finance professional and found I kept having the same conversations over and over again, I wanted to dig deeper to understand why most people aren't good with money. Good money management is not just a learned skill that is almost never taught anymore; it's also an understanding that we will always be our own worst enemies.

This book isn't about economics, though I do have an honours degree in the subject. It's about understanding how our psychology affects our behaviour with money. We all stumble into our own ways of doing things and then arbitrarily decide if it's working for us or not without ever really testing any alternatives. I've been refining the process I describe in this book by practising new approaches with Kelly and people like Daniel and Susan over the years, reading books and watching videos on the psychology of money and sharing what I learn along the way.

One of my heroes is Daniel Kahneman, a world-renowned psychologist and recipient of the Nobel Prize for economics for his groundbreaking work on prospect theory, which is considered to be the foundation of behavioural economics. If you haven't read Kahneman's international bestseller *Thinking, Fast and Slow*, I highly recommend you do. It's quite a thick book, but it's filled with great ideas. One of the central concepts is that the way we think is not what we think thinking is. Let me repeat that:

> The way we think is not what we think thinking is.

Our brains tend to do lots and lots of automatic or intuitive thinking, which Kahneman calls 'System 1' thinking. This is in contrast to the much more effortful, logical and analytical 'System 2' thinking, which is what we think thinking is. To understand the difference between the two, consider the simple problem Kahneman poses:

> If a bat and ball together cost $1.10, but the ball costs $1 less than the bat, how much does the ball cost?

The answer that immediately comes to mind is 10 cents, but that's wrong. Around 50% of people, when asked this question, won't bother thinking beyond their intuitive, *fast* answer or checking to see if they're correct. This is System 1 thinking at work. However, if the ball is 10 cents and the bat is a dollar more, then the bat would be $1.10 and the combined cost would be $1.20 – so the answer '10 cents' has to be wrong. The correct answer is five cents. If the ball is five cents and the bat is a dollar more, that would be $1.05, plus five cents is $1.10. To work it out properly requires effort, which is System 2, *slow* thinking.

We spend most of our lives using the fast, intuitive System 1 thinking because it saves us time and energy. System 2 thinking is much slower and requires much more effort, which our brain tries avoid whenever possible. In a world where food was scarce, evolution helped us to keep out of trouble by making fast decisions to conserve energy by not engaging our whole brain every minute of every day. Yet we all have the ability to use System 2 thinking, so we naturally assume the rest of our thoughts are just as rational as we feel we are. This is a good foundation to keep in mind as you progress through this book.

My story

In my early career I worked for a huge manufacturer of fast-moving consumer goods typically found in supermarkets. The category I was responsible for, washing powder, was the most unprofitable part of their business, because it's a very competitive market. The thinking within the business was that washing powder only sells when it's on promotion, that people wait for the promotions before they buy. However, my observation was that although it would be rational for consumers to buy only when the price of powder is the cheapest, not everyone works like that.

Shopping for specials was the behaviour that I personally exhibited. However, when Kelly went shopping, she didn't care what was on special. Her favourite brand is Omo, so she would buy Omo. She liked the 1 kg packs, so she would buy the 1 kg pack even if the 1.5 kg pack was on special at the same price as the 1 kg with a big ticket saying '50% EXTRA FREE'. She simply wouldn't see the promotions because she was only looking for the 1 kg pack of Omo.

Hunting for specials is the rational way to shop. It makes sense to me and other tight-arses, but Kelly's behaviour represents the majority. Imagine how much slower and more exhausting a shopping trip would be if we all shopped for every item in the rational way: scanning the whole shelf, looking for the right quality at the right price.

When I dug a bit deeper, I found that in a supermarket, there is a certain level of sales that happens for every single product, regardless of what else is going on around them. In the super-competitive, highly promoted category of washing powder, non-promoted products still account for around 50% of all sales. The other 50% of sales come from people just switching within sizes of the same brand to get whatever's on special at that time, or switching within a cluster of brands to get whichever is cheapest. However, retailers were much smarter than consumers. They would only buy when manufacturers were offering a special and then fill up their warehouses, knowing that they could sell the discounted goods to their customers at full price when the manufacturers' promotion ended.

In 2001, I ran a year-long experiment, stopping most promotional activities. Instead, I introduced wonderfully priced promotional packs that were deliberately designed to attract the attention of the rational, promotion-hungry buyers such as myself. I left the rest of the products at full price, both to retailers and customers, so that people like my wife would end up spending more in the supermarket. For the company, this was brilliant. It went from losing millions of dollars on washing powder to making millions. Although I got promoted as a result, I didn't feel great about it, and I eventually left that company and career to become a teacher.

I've always loved teaching. I love the art of helping someone understand a concept or process that at first seemed unfathomable to them. However, when I moved back to Australia with my family in 2009, the NSW Department of Education didn't like my UK qualification, so I turned my hand to finance. This is where I found my true calling, because people really need a financial education – and I've made providing that education my mission.

At my company Golden Eggs, I now use the same psychological principles that I used back in my early career, those so well-articulated by Kahneman, to help normal people manage their money better. Every day, I help people save more, pay debt down faster and spend on things that make them happier – all without experiencing the money worries that are familiar to so many people all over the world, regardless of how high their income is.

This book

I'm not a psychologist, but I have spent most of my adult life adding value to the work that I do by understanding that people are different and changeable – and not only that people are different to one another, but also that their behaviour is often different to what they think their behaviour is. My ambition with this book is to show you how to relax and let your System 1 thinking take the reins most of the time, while setting up barriers to prevent overspending and trigger System 2 thinking when System 1 is leading you astray.

Drawing inspiration from groundbreaking works of behavioural economics and psychology, the first part of *Spending, Fast and Slow* explores the intricacies of human decision-making and uncovers the cognitive biases and heuristics that lead people astray when it comes to spending. Then, through a blend of practical advice, relatable anecdotes and research, I'll help you uncover the mental traps that may be holding you back or causing stress. I delve into impulse buying, the power of advertising and the modern monetary system, highlighting the invisible forces that shape our financial choices. From there, I move on to practical strategies for budgeting, saving to invest and saving to spend, showing you how to apply these principles to create a solid financial foundation.

In these early chapters, I'm going to coach you to deliberately engage your System 2 thinking. This means starting to plan and set some goals for what you want to do with your money in the future to help you prioritise the way you use it today. There'll always be a gap between what you think you're doing and what you're actually doing, and it's important to understand why that gap exists to try and make sure that you don't repeat the mistakes of the past. Central to this is understanding that the way your finances are set up can encourage you to spend *fast*, using the intuitive side of your brain, or more *slowly* and thoughtfully and on the things that are a priority for you.

In the second part of this book, I'll walk you through the Fast and Slow System, which separates money into different buckets with different banks to make it as difficult as possible to fall victim to fast spending. I've been coaching this system since 2011 (and using it myself since 2004), so I know it works. I'll also support you to tailor your system to your unique personality and goals, because I've learned that if the outcome isn't tailored to the way the individual operates then it's just not going to fly. More importantly, unless we can learn from others and implement a better system, we're always going to struggle with money – or be far less efficient with it than we could be. To help you with this, I'm going to give you support around several common problems and barriers that many people face when learning to being good with money – the biggest of which is credit cards.

The final phase is about execution, but that's about more than just implementing the Fast and Slow System. It's also about how you live and enjoy your life. The funny thing is, what makes people happiest is helping and connecting with others and having treats and experiences, not spending money on stuff. I'm going to look at that in more detail in the final chapter, because what

I really want is for you to have a great and happy life – not just be the richest person in the graveyard.

To help our clients manage their money using the Fast and Slow System, the Golden Eggs team has built a web app, located at app.goldeneggs.info. This app walks users through the process of setting up and managing a spending plan – everything from personality combinations and long-term goal setting to calculations for spending, paying down a mortgage and hitting savings goals. You may find it a helpful support as you read and implement the ideas in this book. Plus, it can be integrated with your Australian bank accounts to extract spending data before and after you set up a spending plan. It's accessible (with all the features) for the first month at no charge. One day it'll be a downloadable app, but as of 2023 it's fully online and best viewed via desktop rather than on a phone.

As you progress through all three parts of *Spending, Fast and Slow*, you'll begin to see your relationship with money in a new light and, with this newfound understanding, be better equipped to make choices that align with your values and goals. This book is an invitation to a life of greater financial awareness, resilience and freedom – a life in which money becomes a tool for achieving your dreams rather than an ever-present source of stress.

So, take a deep breath. Let's embark on this journey together. Here's to a future of spending more slowly, and to the richer, more fulfilling life that awaits you.

PART I

HARNESSING YOUR MIND FOR A RICHER LIFE

PART I

HARNESSING YOUR MIND FOR A RICHER LIFE

Chapter 1

A brief history of money and the elimination of friction

The way that money works in the world today has a real effect on our lives, so to understand why so many people – regardless of their income – aren't as good with money as they'd like to be, first we need to look at where money has come from and where it is now. As you'll see, changes in technology have played a large role in our changing relationship with money over the years and continue to contribute to the difficulties that many of us experience, particularly from a psychological perspective. Having laid this foundation, in coming chapters we'll find ways to work with modern technology to reach our goals.

The evolution of money

Money is thought to have started off as shells, but since around 700 BCE metal coins, sometimes gold and silver, have been used. People were paid in physical money that they carried with them. They had that feeling of carrying around a bag full of something that felt valuable. When they went to spend their money, they were handing over something that they valued. Psychologically, they felt that pain.

From the 17th century, larger values could be represented by paper notes, so people had folding money that they could put in their pockets. More folding money could be carried around, but it could easily be burnt or damaged in some way, so people were less attached to it. Paper money was hard to bury or hide away because, unlike coins, paper would physically deteriorate, so it became more common for people to put money they didn't want to spend in 'safe' places like banks.

Banks wanted to hold onto money for as long as possible, so they gave people the option to use cheques. Suddenly, people could just write a number on a piece of paper to spend that amount. From a psychological perspective, when people wrote a cheque, they knew that to be operating within the law they had to have at least as much in their account as they were intending to spend. There was always a bit of a lag, typically five days, between when cheques were paid and the money came out of your bank account. That meant people had to cross reference the cheques that they'd written against their bank balance. It also meant that cheques weren't always backed up by what was in someone's bank account, but the person receiving the cheque didn't necessarily know that. (That's when we get stories about people writing cheques that couldn't be cashed.)

In 1950, Frank McNamara and Ralph Schneider introduced the Diners Club Card – the first modern credit card – as a way of helping young men avoid the embarrassment of going out to dinner and finding they were expected to pay for a meal, the cost of which may have gotten out of hand, and not being able to. Avoiding being unable to pay is one of the fundamental benefits that people still see in credit cards today.

By the mid-'60s, bank accounts could be linked to cards, superseding the need to write a cheque in many instances, with signature verification required for each transaction. In 1972 personal identification numbers were introduced in the UK to allow people to access their money and pay for what they wanted without signatures, but it took until 2014 before signatures were phased out in Australia, and many US outlets still use signatures today.

In the '60s and '70s, people went from being paid in cash weekly to being paid by cheque, requiring employees to have a bank account to pay their cheques into. Then, during the '80s and '90s, direct deposits replaced cheques, meaning employers could automate transfers to bank accounts instead of printing pages of cheques and physically handing them over on payday. Banks used to charge a fee per cheque or transfer, so employers realised they could halve their fees by paying fortnightly. Some even went to monthly pay cycles. Suddenly, we not only had access to all our money at once but also had to make it last from two to five weeks instead of only one – a double whammy!

Now that we've got tap and go, we just tap our cards, phones or watches. We don't always pay attention to what we're doing, either – we just get what we want and there's some sort of reconciliation at the bank. There's no pain of paying for things, no sense of loss that we're giving up something we earned for goods or services. We don't even need to know how much money we actually have to be able to spend it! All our money is just abstract digits in a computer system somewhere.

It has become extremely difficult to keep track of our money, particularly when compared to the days of coins or even paper money. Before we zero in on how we spend money today, I want to take a moment to explore how people used to manage their money, which is knowledge that seems to have disappeared over generations.

Money-management strategies of the recent past

Before 1970, when cash dominated, people knew that carrying all your money around with you was going to cause problems. The metaphor of money 'burning a hole in your pocket' is common for a reason! The idea is that if you carry a lot of coins, soon they'll all be gone and you won't know where the money went – almost like they've disappeared through a hole in your pocket. Spending or losing all your money was understood to be a function of how much you chose to carry around with you.

For generations, everyone knew that you had to protect your wealth, and the first and most obvious way of doing that was hiding it away. For example, you might have heard of grandparents keeping a tin of bank notes and change in the kitchen, burying a stash in the garden or tucking money under the mattress. The bottom line was this: when you went out and about, you would never take all your money.

In addition to not carrying around all their cash, here are some successful strategies people used in the past (and a minority still use today) to reduce their spending on less important things:

1. **Rationing** – This looks like giving yourself just a little bit of money when you go out while keeping most of your money at home. This usually meant money would last until more came in.
2. **Bank accounts** – Only wealthy people had bank accounts in the early days, and then they became a place to put savings – literally keeping money safe. Eventually, all savings and pay were put directly into bank accounts, but even then, most people drew cash from their accounts as they only spent the money they had on them. Money in bank accounts

couldn't really be touched until the advent of cheques and debit cards.

3. **Investing** – Investing is still considered one of the best ways of hiding money from ourselves. Putting money into something that is likely to grow in the future, whether that be in a friend's business, shares or property, is a way to know that the money is now gone and can't be spent.
4. **Buying a home** – You might have heard of mortgages being described as 'forced savings'. A mortgage is normally a principal-and-interest loan; the interest is the cost of borrowing the money from the bank, which is much like rent, but the principal is the amount being paid off. Mortgages force us to reduce our amount of debt over time, saving us money in the future.
5. **Allocating financial control** – Often in relationships, one person is better with money than the other. This strategy sees the person with the best head for money take control of both parties' finances. Of course, there is the possibility of financial abuse within this strategy, but when done willingly and with consent it can work very well as a tactic to ensure a household's money doesn't just disappear.

My parents' story

My parents used a few of these strategies to manage their finances. My dad left home at 16 in 1959 and worked on farms. He realised by the time he met my mum at 20 that he was no good with money. He would just spend any money in his pocket. He just wasn't very good at keeping track of it. He'd always end up with problems. He might go to the pub planning to just have one drink, and then one turned into two, which turned into three. Before he knew it, he'd spent half his pay.

When he got married, he said to my mum 'I'm no good with money' and handed over his pay to her each week. As I've mentioned, it was common back then for one person in the relationship to take on the role of money manager and save the other from thinking about it. Unlike my dad, my mum was very good with money.

Like any good household manager, my mother knew that in addition to the weekly expenses, money was needed for the less regular expenses like the mortgage, electricity and other bills – even the coal bill. Believe it or not, coal could be delivered a few times a year, and you would have to have enough money to buy half a ton or more of coal to be able to feed the fire all winter.

My mum realised quickly that money had to be separated out. She had two purses: one that she carried with her and one that sat in the cupboard at home. Each had separate compartments. She had different sections for the milkman's bill, the paper bill, council rates and other bills that were coming up. Mum knew that any money she had in the purse she carried around was OK to spend, and my dad knew that when he went out he had to ask my mum for money.

As they dealt exclusively in physical money, it was clear to my mum exactly how much money was available to manage the household, and my dad could only spend the money he was given. Mum was able to make sure all their bills got paid, their nine children were all fed and clothed, the whole family went on holiday every year and the house was being paid off. This worked both because my mum did a great job and also because my dad acknowledged his own failings with money and accepted that he was unlikely to be able to change.

Their use of cash, which was really the only option at the time, was also important to their success. There've been numerous studies from around the world that show if you use cash, you will spend up until the point when you've run out of cash, but you'll also make that cash last much longer than when using digital money. It wasn't until much later that they got bank accounts and debit cards. Even then they still did things the same way. Mum was responsible for the finances and would either transfer money to my dad or draw out the cash.

Money today

Not all the strategies of yesteryear work today. Our world is just too different. These days, everything we do is tap and go. It's all electronic. Many of us opened our first bank accounts when we got our first job, so we've never received a physical pay packet. Our wages were paid into a bank account, we had a bank card to access it and away we went. Some of us even got our first bank account when we were children! Even bank cards have evolved – we've got them on our phones and watches now, because who can remember to carry both a wallet and a phone around?

In many ways, life is much better, and we love the convenience of being able to access money in so many different ways. Unfortunately, this convenience is where a lot of money problems stem from. Additionally, we don't really know what we're spending. We aren't handing over physical coins or cash, so we don't feel the sense of loss I described earlier in this chapter. Our spending is so abstract that many of us can only track it after the fact instead of at the point of purchase. Just think about it for a second. Try to recall the last time you spent money using your card and how much you spent.

If you think about the way that we pay now, we're normally handed a payWave terminal without being told how much we're about to pay. The other day I went to the pub and bought a couple of drinks. It probably came to $20 or so. The cashier didn't say the number aloud, and I then placed a card on the terminal, over the amount that I had to pay – *without even looking*. I was literally hiding the amount I was paying. I didn't hear the amount and didn't see it!

It's not just me, either. A few years back, an Australian cricket correspondent was buying a beer in a pub in England and was accidentally charged £55,000. Amazingly, the transaction went through, and it was only afterwards that he realised. The staff member lost their job and it took weeks of negotiation for the correspondent to get the exchange-rate difference back.

Think about that and what you normally do. It's fantastic for businesses to make it so easy for us, but psychologically, how can we keep track of spending when it's all so opaque?

The elimination of friction

We're now so divorced from the money we spend that many people have started to use spend-tracking apps. A lot of banks provide them, plus there are third-party apps like Frollo that can aggregate information across multiple accounts. These apps analyse transactions, categorise them and then try to give users an idea of how much they've spent on different things.

So, we've gone from knowing that every time we handed over money it was coming out of our hard-earned wages, to now having to look back after the fact to see where it all went. The brilliant thing about this for people selling stuff is that spending is now frictionless.

Friction is a force that slows or stops something from moving forward. Instead of reaching into your pocket for another bag of coins and physically handing something over, going back home to look in the tin box or heading to the bank to get the cash – all of which give us time to use System 2 thinking – it's just 'Yes, please', tap and go. There's no delay between the thought of wanting something and getting it. It's a wonderful thing for businesses, salespeople and marketers but not so wonderful for us.

We make hundreds of tiny financial decisions every day using System 1 thinking, and money seems to just disappear. We can look up what we've done online, but the pain of paying for something is now almost non-existent. We just get a little dopamine hit when we buy things. This will keep happening, over and over, until we realise that we're either not saving as much as we think we should or we get in way over our heads – and that can lead to a crisis point.

Many people can go their entire working lives spending most of their income and thinking everything is fine, until their income suddenly stops. This hurt a lot of people during the COVID-19 lockdowns, but in normal times it's often triggered by sudden retrenchment or retirement. When your income drops to $27,664 ($41,704 for a couple) on the Age Pension, for example, it's a shock to realise that living on $150,000 a year was easy in comparison. If you think this could never happen to you, then consider the long-term consequences of always spending more than you need to on things you don't value. As you'll see in forthcoming chapters, adding this friction back in at specific points could help us spend less, while automating other processes can help us save more. In chapter 10, for example, you'll find the story of how Rob and Claire, who thought they were doing fine, were able to cut 10 years off their mortgage, simply by re-introducing friction and automating their savings.

Summary

- The nature of money has fundamentally changed over time. Today, it's so abstract that we don't even look at what we're spending until after the fact.
- Cash is easier to manage and can be hidden away to make spending harder, and it lets us feel the pain of paying for things.
- Contactless payments remove the friction that might slow down our spending and decouple the pain of paying from the transaction.
- Managing money is now often done in hindsight, using apps, rather than at the point of purchase or beforehand.
- Modern banking systems have almost eliminated friction in our lives, and purposefully re-introducing that friction can help us manage our money better.

Chapter 2

Money, happiness and decision-making

Can money buy happiness?

After seeing where money has come from and how difficult it is to manage in a digital world, it's worth now spending some time to understand whether we become happier when we spend more. There's no consistent measure for happiness over time, although we can refer to the World Happiness Report for some indication. The 2022 report shows Australia is ranked 12th in the world with an average score of 7.09/10 over 2019 to 2021. Compare this to the score of the leading country, Finland, which was 7.8/10 for the same period, and to Australia's own 2013 score of 7.35/10.

To understand money and happiness, we first need to understand how our brains work – and they don't always work the way we think they do. In this chapter, we'll return to Kahneman's two different systems of thinking and explore how it translates to spending decisions and behaviour. Once we have a better idea of how we think, we can then begin to explore common money worries, which often come down to misapplication of the two systems of thinking and our resulting behaviour. This is very relevant to happiness, because it's hard to be happy when we're worried about stuff!

Being in a long-term, loving relationship is closely correlated with happiness, but money is often listed as one of the top five reasons for breakdowns of relationships. It put serious stress on my own marriage for over a decade before my wife and I got our heads around our different money personalities and implemented a system that put our family finances in a much healthier state, allowing us both to become much happier.

Thinking (and spending), fast and slow

As I mentioned in the introduction, *Thinking, Fast and Slow* by Daniel Kahneman is a fantastic book, and I cannot recommend it highly enough. Kahneman is a leader in behavioural economics, which focuses on the link between psychology – the study of the mind and the way that we behave – and the economics of our society, and his book explores policy and big-picture decision-making that can help society as a whole. In this book, *Spending, Fast and Slow*, I take a slightly different approach, delving deeper into what we can do as individuals to manage our money. Before we can get into that, however, we need to better understand how brains work. I shared a little about this in the introduction to this book, briefly explaining Kahneman's two systems of thinking:

- System 1 – the fast, instant and automatic thinking where we're not really thinking at all, which is how most of our decisions are actually made
- System 2 – the slow, deliberate style of thinking that aligns with most of our identities as clear-thinking, rational adults.

Most people identify as clear-thinking, intelligent, rational human beings, and for the most part they are right. However, thinking requires effort, and as human beings we try to find ways to avoid exerting effort while getting the same outcomes. This means most of the time, instead of using the effortful System 2 thinking, we use System 1 thinking, which is automatic and tends to run in response to triggers.

This isn't necessarily a bad thing. Sometimes we need to act urgently (when we're in danger, for example), so our brain gives us the ability to respond quickly. This typically means doing automatically what we've practised before or what we think will get us out of danger quickest.

An example of one such trigger is fear. If we see something that could be dangerous and we experience fear, we immediately act to get ourselves to safety. From an evolutionary standpoint, for instance, we wouldn't have wanted to waste time pondering the pros and cons of running away from a sabre-toothed tiger!

Another trigger is hunger. When we're hungry, we know, even without thinking about it consciously, that we need to eat. Suddenly, we're going through the cupboards or the fridge and eating something – sometimes without really being aware that we're doing it. We don't always make a considered decision to start eating.

Another example of System 1 thinking is when we're driving a car and suddenly realise that we've arrived home but don't remember what happened on the way. During that time, our brains were looking out for signals, such as red lights and other cars, and reacting to those signals while also drifting off into other thoughts. We weren't conscious of the fact that we were making these little decisions on the way, but our brains were able to keep us safe anyway.

We see the same effect with spending money. Returning to the food example, when we're out and about somewhere and feel hungry, many people buy snacks instead of just waiting until they get home. There have even been many studies proving that the best way of reducing your grocery bill is to have a nice big meal and a big drink before you go shopping, because if you go shopping when you're hungry and thirsty you're likely to load your trolley full of things that you can quickly drink or eat. Studies have also shown that we get a little dopamine hit when we go shopping, even before we've bought anything, so sometimes when we're feeling a bit down we end up going shopping; we're simply acting in a way that will make us feel a bit better.

According to Harvard Professor Gerald Zaltman, 95% of our decisions about spending money are made subconsciously, without that effortful, purposeful System 2 thinking. Imagine for a moment that you want a big-ticket item – for example, a car. You would probably think very carefully about the amount of money that you want to spend, the type of car that you want and the features that are most important to you. You're likely to look at all sorts of pros and cons of different models before you finally make that purchase. (Even then, car salespeople are trained to tap into your emotions to sell you on the idea and prestige of a $70,000 car while focusing on the relatively low weekly cost of only $260.) You're not going to put the same effort into buying a soft drink, a snack or a simple T-shirt. With those smaller items we deem to be less consequential, we can move very quickly from the thought *I would like this* to the action of buying it without really looking at the money impacts of that decision.

The net result of this is that although we may think of ourselves as sane, sensible, rational people, if we listed all our purchases for the last month most would just be habitual or impulse buys.

We rationalise each at the time and feel that every individual transaction is probably OK, but when we add up all the money spent on those small, quick things, it's likely to be much more than was spent on the memorable things. For example, we remember signing up to a phone plan, paying the rent or a big electricity bill and making a car repayment, but not the hot chips on the way home. This means that even when we think of economising, we focus on the big things and not on the hundreds of small things, regardless of how much those small things are actually costing us.

Studies show that we tend to assess whether or not to spend according to our account balance. When we have $5000 in the bank, a $500 spending decision feels significant and worthy of thought, whereas a $30 spending decision seems too trivial to think about. As we'll see later, the more money we can access, the more likely we are to see most expenses as trivial and the more we spend. This can make us feel we're not getting ahead and give us plenty to worry about if we're not careful.

Money worries

Over 70% of us worry about money to some extent. However, there are different levels to that worry:

- **Level 1** is a mild concern that we're not really getting where we want to and we're not really achieving our money goals.
- **Level 2** is when we think, *Oh my goodness, I spent too much money this month*, or when we don't have enough money left to do something we want to. It feels like we're in problem-solving mode: how do we get enough money to do what we want?
- **Level 3** is when we've gotten behind. Maybe we've missed a credit card bill, we've lost a job or something has happened

that means we suddenly don't have as much money as we thought. Now we have to struggle to get back to where we want to be.

- **Level 4** is a dire, deep hole of debt. Maybe we've tried rolling over credit card balances to get an interest free period, but then we've run up another big bill. Maybe something else might happen that means we're not paying our bills at all. This is a very serious problem that requires urgent and immediate action.

Recovering from the fourth level of money worry will almost certainly require professional help, which is not what this book is designed to provide. This book is designed to help people recover from the first three levels of money worry and avoid the fourth altogether.

It's hard to be happy when you're worried, even if some areas of your life are in sync. Money worries distract you from enjoying where you are in life, so you need to set up a system that gives you the confidence to not worry. My goal with this whole book is to help you to stop thinking about money (most of the time), which is exactly what your brain wants to do.

Money and relationships

There are many reasons why relationships break down, but the two issues that I know how to resolve are a lack of shared goals and problems with money. We'll talk about setting goals in chapter 4, which is essential to do as a joint exercise if you're in a couple, but first I want to explore money problems and how they can make a relationship become bitter and resentful – and even cause a complete breakdown.

My wife Kelly and I have been married for more than three decades, but money was a constant source of arguments for the first 11 years. My natural tendency is to be a tight-arse, which is in complete opposition to my wife, who is a natural shopaholic. If we earned it or saved it, she would find a way to spend it, and over time our vastly different approaches to, and expectations about, money started to cause serious arguments.

One of our biggest ongoing problems was the use of a credit card (more on the dangers of credit cards in chapter 10). Every year I would do a budget and estimate our expected savings, but every year we would miss our goal – and by a long way. Month to month, there was always a reason why the credit card bill was a bit bigger than anticipated. It was the holidays, the kids were going back to school, or the car registration or some other big bill was due. However, if we'd bothered to look at the detail of each credit card bill, we would've seen it was actually the hundreds of little expenses that were pushing us over budget. I know now that when we were reviewing the bills, we were using System 1 thinking to quickly identify the big-ticket items and assume that they were the problem, rather than engaging System 2 thinking to realise that those bigger expenses were in the original budget. As is the case for most people, when life is busy (particularly with kids), taking a detailed look at the credit card bill felt like too much effort.

So, how did we get through it? We implemented the Fast and Slow System (explored in detail in chapter 7): we stopped using credit cards, separated our bank accounts and adjusted the timing of deposits. Once we changed the way we managed money, the arguments all but stopped. The shopaholic was given more autonomy with her money, the tight-arse had no ability to check what things were costing, and together we spent way less money.

This is based on simple psychology. When the two of us were spending from the same account, it was easy to blame each other for problems that arose. When we each spent from our own accounts, we each had to hold ourselves – not one another – accountable for what we spent. The tight-arse doesn't need as much money as the shopaholic to be happy.

Additionally, the tight-arse is happier if they can't see what the shopaholic is spending. I've always been a very observant person, and whenever my wife got a new haircut, new outfit, or piece of jewellery, my first question was, 'How much did that cost?' The outcome was perfectly predictable: Kelly felt bad and made excuses, and I felt more and more stressed about where all our money was going. Now, with a fixed budget to work from, instead of hiding purchases (or putting part of a purchase on the card and using cash for the rest) Kelly finds creative ways of using the funds within her budget to get what she wants.

Importantly, I never question the cost of something, and I don't stress over it. We can now even laugh about the creativity Kelly used to get what she wanted. The way we're set up now, if she shows up in something new, all I say is, 'That looks nice!' because I don't care what it cost. There is a budget, it's within budget, therefore it's OK. If she thinks it's important enough for her to buy, then it's not my business how much she spends, and vice versa.

As a tight-arse, it was initially very hard for me to make this shift. First, I had to understand Kelly's money personality as a shopaholic, as well as my own as a tight-arse. Then, I had to show compassion for and accept each of our natural tendencies. Not everyone was raised with no money and trained, as I was, to believe that *things* aren't worth buying. Rather, most people grow up with the understanding that nice things will make them feel good or show their value and worth to society. The solution for me was not to tighten the reins or embody Ebenezer Scrooge of Charles Dickens's *A Christmas Carol*. Instead, I had to do one of the most difficult things for tight-arses to do: relinquish control of money, let go and allow my partner to feel free to spend.

In short, both the shopaholic and the tight-arse needed to adapt their behaviour to become happy. With each of us sticking to the plan – accountable for our own actions and with the autonomy to spend a specific amount as we pleased, no questions asked – family finances thrived. For a shopaholic to work consistently to a budget (over many years now) and for a tight-arse to let go were huge but necessary changes, and they made a real difference to the health of our relationship.

Vanessa and Jason

When I first met Vanessa and Jason, they were saving to buy their first home, except they weren't really saving at all. Both had good incomes in professional fields and, in theory, they should've been able to save their deposit in two or three years. In practice, when we deducted Jason's personal loans, car loan and credit card debt from Vanessa's savings, they were in a negative position.

This situation is not uncommon. People think they're saving, but they're also signing up for car loans, spending on credit cards and borrowing money to go on holidays. I met Vaness and Jason when I was a mortgage broker, and I hadn't yet developed the tools and techniques of a money coach. All I could see was that they needed to save more money and reduce their debts, which would take more time. We agreed to have another chat in six months or so when they had their savings together.

Unfortunately, I didn't hear from the two of them again – that is, until Vanessa approached me saying that she was looking to buy a place for herself and her daughter to live in because she'd separated from Jason. It turned out that his inability to curb his spending and pay down debts led Vanessa to believe she had no choice but to end the relationship. She still cared for Jason – he's the father of their daughter and they saw each other regularly – but the relationship was over. I can't help but feel bad, even today, because if I had known then what I know now, maybe I could have helped them implement a better structure that would have put the two of them on a similar footing to my wife and I.

If you're reading this and you're in a relationship with someone with whom you are arguing about money, please persevere – not just with the relationship but also with the rest of this book, because I genuinely want to help. I want people to experience the kind of long-term relationship that I've had, where you find a way to overcome difficult times together.

Thankfully, Vanessa was able to buy a place with her savings and moved forward with her life, together with her daughter, feeling much more confident about money. More recently, she has reached out to me again to talk about her shared goals and buying a home with her new partner.

Spending in ways that make you happy

Another wonderful book worth reading is *Happy Money*. The authors, psychologists Elizabeth Dunn and Michael Norton, examined existing studies and ran many of their own to find out what makes us happy when it comes to spending money. They make five key findings that we can apply to how we spend money in ways that will maximise happiness.

First, **experiences make us happy, not things**. This isn't just bungy jumping or flying in a hot air balloon; it's also spending time with friends and family, going for a walk and doing simple yet meaningful things, either by ourselves or with others. For me, that includes playing football, seeing a great sunset, walking to work and hugging my kids and grandson. On the other hand, buying new things give us a brief high that makes us feel happy only temporarily. Studies and experience tell us that within a very short space of time, the new thing becomes just one of our things and stops making us feel happy, or we simply find that the thing doesn't live up to our expectations. Sometimes we even regret our purchases, resulting in a phenomenon known as 'buyer's remorse'.

Dunn and Norton's second finding is that **making something a treat increases our enjoyment of it**. This means both enjoying daily habits less often and doing bigger things in smaller doses more often. A morning barista-made coffee may be enjoyable, but having one daily reduces the pleasure we get from it. Instead, if we get our caffeine fix by making it ourselves most days and treat ourselves to proper coffee only occasionally, we appreciate it way more. Bigger items work the other way around. For example, a 90-minute massage might sound amazing if you like that kind of thing. However, a 30-minute massage might give you almost as much pleasure and could be enjoyed two or three times for the same cost.

The next suggestion for increasing our happiness is to **out-source chores to buy time**. Chores, like worries, are things that detract from happiness. Spending money having someone else do the ironing or mow the lawn, or investing in technology such as a Roomba to reduce the load, can help us relax and frees up time for us to enjoy ourselves more.

The authors also found that **saving for things increases the anticipation and pleasure we derive from it**. The pleasure we gain in anticipating a purchase is greater that the pleasure brought by the purchase itself. Studies even show that we are happier in the weeks leading up to a holiday than when we're actually on the holiday. The opposite is also true: using credit cards and personal loans to buy stuff instantly not only robs us of the pleasure of looking forward to something but also leaves us with stress and worry afterwards. Saving for a holiday makes us feel like we're already on the way, months in advance of the trip itself. Ironically, even if the holiday itself is bad, we'll enjoy telling the stories if we don't have a credit card hangover.

Finally, **buying for others makes us happier than buying for ourselves**. Human beings are social animals, and we love getting acceptance and approval from others. Great ways of doing this include buying gifts, shouting a round or picking up the bill at the end of a meal. Other people's happiness is contagious, so when we see the smile of someone we've just given a gift to, we feel happy. It also deepens our connection with that person. Some of the richest people in the world have realised this as they've gotten older and wiser. Bill Gates and Warren Buffett, for example, are both determined to give away 99% of their wealth before they die (visit givingpledge.org for more information). Even my mum, who was never wealthy, would cheer herself up by giving her savings away to her kids periodically. It never mattered to her if any of us were wealthier or more financially stable; if she gave £100 to one of us in dire need of some help, she would give £100 to all nine children. This was usually staggered over time to get the best response from each of us and keep her on that high from giving.

This is just my summary of a brilliant book that I believe is well worth the read. Not only are the authors' findings and suggestions backed by psychological research, but I've also found them to be true in my own experience. With all these ideas, it's important to return to the idea that if you stay within the budget that you've set yourself, these five ways of spending are shown to make people happier than other forms might. Consider *Happy Money*, then, as a reminder when creating your own spending plan to put more emphasis on categories likely to make you happy than those that leave you flat.

Summary

- Being happy always starts with removing barriers to happiness. One common barrier is money worries, and these worries can have serious effects on relationships. If we can get those worries under control, then we can focus on spending money in ways that make us happier.
- Most money decisions are made automatically or with System 1 thinking, which means money disappears quickly if we're not careful.
- Money worries can vary from mild to dire. Our aim is to eliminate all worries and significantly reduce the amount of time spent thinking about money at all.
- Many couples have money arguments, so it's important to understand each other's money personalities and adapt ways of working to suit both. If differences in money personalities aren't properly understood and addressed, loving relationships can end due to the resulting money issues.
- Beyond basic needs, focusing spending on experiences, treats, outsourcing chores, things we've saved for and gifts for others can make us happier than just buying things for ourselves or for instant gratification.

Chapter 3
Understanding money

Most of us like to think that we're in control of our money. We think we know what we spend. We think we know how much we can save and believe ourselves to be sane, sensible adults. Effectively, our intuition, or System 1 thinking, tells us that we're good enough with money. However, the statistics tell a different story. Over the past 50 years, basic costs for survival living in Australia have dropped from over 60% of our income to under 50%, yet our savings rate over the same period has fallen from between 15 and 20% to under 5%. That means our spending on non-essentials has risen from between 20 and 25% to between 40 and 45% of our income. But why? And where is all that extra money going?

Why is money hard to master?

The truth is that money is hard to master, for three main reasons:

1. Temptation is difficult to resist.
2. Access to money is too easy.
3. Mental maths is tough.

Temptation

Imagine you eat all your meals at an all-you-can-eat buffet. You know that you need a sensible breakfast, a modest lunch, maybe a snack in the afternoon and a reasonable dinner. However, if a wide variety of tempting food was on display at every mealtime, I'm sure most of us would throw an extra thing on our plate, maybe to try something new, because our eyes are bigger than our bellies or because we feel that it doesn't really matter. If you've ever been on a cruise or stayed at an all-inclusive resort, you'll know that you can't help but eat way too much at breakfast, way too much at lunch and way too much at dinner.

It's the same with money. Temptation is everywhere, and advertisers and marketers are paid big dollars (and spend millions) to grab our attention and make us think that we want things – and in unexpected ways. One of the most bizarre statistics that I found in my research for this book is that if a shop plays slow music, people spend 38% more in that shop than if they played no music at all! Additionally, if the songs are familiar, we may spend less, while we spend more if they're unfamliar. Additionally, slow music subconsciously tells us to slow down and browse more. The more we slow down and look, the higher the probability that we will give in to temptation. Almost everyone thinks they're in complete control of their actions, that they're not a person who buys something they weren't planning to, but these studies show that's just not true.

Online it is even more tempting to spend money. There are systems and tricks everywhere these days, with cross-site tracking, social media marketing and algorithms that link everything together to cleverly target you with ads for just what you might want. Think about when you've been consuming content or looking up something and suddenly you see ads for that same thing in your social media feeds. Marketers will pay a fortune to learn if you're the kind of person who is interested in their product and get you ever closer to the point of purchase. Before much of our lives went online, this was done using basic demographics such as gender, marital status, location, age and media consumption. These days, it's a much smarter operation that incorporates all sorts of data to target people with specific attitudes (even certain political leanings), likes and dislikes, and aspirations, so they can be tempted most effectively.

Access

We have access to our money via our cards, phones and watches all the time. An interesting psychological trait that we all have when it comes to any type of resource is the fear of scarcity. When a resource is scarce, we treat every use of that resource as difficult and painful, and we use that resource very carefully. When a resource appears abundant, then we know we're fine to use it for whatever we want, whenever we want.

It's easy to think of this in the context of fresh water or food. If those things are abundant, then we can eat and drink what we want. We can flush away and wash ourselves with fresh, clean water and not feel guilty about it. You might have seen a movie in which people are lost at sea, or in the desert or trapped somewhere with limited amounts of food and water. They survive by rationing to make their resources last. When we have droughts, we're asked to stop watering our gardens and washing our cars, spend less time in the shower and flush sparingly.

A study in the *Journal of Consumer Research* shows it's the same with money. When people are prompted to think about smaller amounts of money, such as how much is in their wallet or their everyday account, they spend significantly less than when they think about their total net worth or life savings.

There are a few psychological processes that are relevant to the funds we can access, which collectively can be called 'mental accounting' – a term I've drawn from the title of Richard H Thaler's article on the subject. Here are three key effects, also drawn from Thaler's article, that I've noticed when working with clients to help them achieve their goals:

- **The framing effect** describes how we see $10 from a budget of $50 as significant and $10 from a $200 budget as trivial. This can result in many small expenses being regarded as trivial relative to the budgeting cycle, which in my experience is normally linked to a pay cycle. Comparing expenses to a large figure such as a monthly pay cycle is more likely to make them seem trivial, meaning more might be wasted on clothes or Uber Eats.
- **The wealth effect** describes how we tend to spend more when we think about or have access to our whole life savings. This is problematic when we do all our banking with one bank and can access all our savings instantly. Another study shows a paradox with a growing trend of moving to daily pay *increasing* feelings of wealth and therefore spending, despite average daily balances being potentially lower. This is consistent with my observations of people who are paid weekly tending to be more wasteful on smaller items, such as bought lunches and soft drinks, than people paid monthly.
- **The source of funds effect** describes how we view money from a bonus or a windfall differently to regular income. People are far more likely to gamble or spend a windfall gain on discretionary items than their regular income.

For most of us, the question is not about having access to $50 of pocket money, because we typically give ourselves access to our entire pay through our debit cards and then access to hundreds (or even thousands) more dollars with our credit cards. This means we're likely to feel we have no reason to be careful with money and that each individual decision to spend won't make much of a difference.

Mental maths

When we do all our banking with one bank and have access to all our pay in one bank account, it's very difficult to keep track of what we're spending. Try this simple exercise. Get out a pen and paper or a blank document or your notes app and answer the following questions:

- Last weekend, what places did you go to?
- How much did you spend at each place?
- How much did you spend in total?

Most people only have a very rough idea about how much they spent. Even those with a great memory struggle to get an accurate figure because they forget the extra little things, such as giving $5 to charity or buying a drink on the way back from the shops.

You might think your banking app keeps track of that for you, but even then, the only way to figure out last weekend's spending is to look at the balance on Friday afternoon and the balance on the following Monday morning and then calculate the difference. Most apps don't tell you what bills or special events are coming up, either, so how do you know whether the amount you spent on the weekend is in line with your budget for the month, the quarter or the year?

Even if you do a full analysis of your spending and resolve to take sandwiches to work to cut back on historically high lunch costs, it's like plugging a hole in a colander: the water will just disappear through another hole. Unless you're looking at the app every single day, you won't know how much things cost.

It all sounds way too hard, and we don't like to do hard stuff, so most of us adopt shortcuts. This is classic System 1 thinking: *Let's find an easy solution that doesn't require a lot of thinking, rather than spending time analysing the problem.* We use these sorts of shortcuts:

- The credit card bill should be around $3000 to $4000 a month. More than that and I need to worry or stop spending.
- I should have at least $1000 left in my bank account at the end of the month.
- I save $1500 as soon as I get paid at the start of the month, then I try to save any leftovers.

People who have a natural tendency to save will probably have an allocation going into their savings account each pay cycle, so they know (or at least they *think*) that what's left in their account should be OK to spend. The difficulty here is that bills aren't synchronised to pay cycles. They come monthly, quarterly and yearly, regardless of whether we're paid weekly, fortnightly or monthly. When I ask people *why* they dip into their savings, they always say that it's to pay for bigger bills (such as medical bills, car registration and insurance), holidays or gifts.

It's very hard to keep track of whether we've just used up all the money we allocated to spend or we needed to keep a certain amount of money back to cover a big bill. If we just had a pay cycle with no bills whatsoever, we'll probably have to dip into savings when all the bills are due the following month. System 1 thinking tells us we're doing that because of all the bills, but System 2 thinking never gets the chance to help us realise the issue was that we spent too much in the first pay cycle.

Going back to the all-you-can-eat buffet, it's all very well to say that we're going to concentrate really hard and be really careful at each and every meal, but how long will that last? Eventually our commitment waivers; something else happens in life that makes us feel a bit bad – or even amazing and like we should treat ourselves. If we're still going to the buffet every day, we know that over the long term we're going to overeat. The only solution is to change where we go to eat and how we access food. The same is true with money.

Getting real

When we put together temptation everywhere, almost unlimited access to our money and an inability to keep track of it all in our heads, it's no wonder that most of us aren't very good with money. Even if you think you're doing OK, almost everyone is worse with money than they think they are. Once we accept this fact about ourselves and understand that we can't really change because we're human, then we can find real solutions to the problem of managing money.

What people say is not what they do

As a mortgage broker, I'm always asking people how much they spend, excluding rent or a mortgage. The reason rent and mortgages are excluded is that most renters are saving to buy a home, at which point the rent disappears, and most people with mortgages want to pay them off as fast as they can. This means we need to look at income less other expenses to figure out how much is available to put towards their mortgage. When we do this, the logical, rational System 2 thinking kicks in and people start doing the bottom-up calculation. I even give out tools to help add everything up. Table 3.1 is a sample of a couple's monthly expenses using this framework. We'll call this couple Lucas and Amy.

Table 3.1: Lucas and Amy's basic expenses per month

Expenses	Cost per month
Electricity	$200
Water	$50
Health insurance	$200
Car insurance	$100
Home insurance	$100
Phone and internet	$150
Groceries	$1400
Car registration	$100
Subtotal	**$2300**

Most people are able to provide fairly accurate figures in these categories. However, for items such as entertainment and clothes, people have no concept of how much they spend, so they estimate. Most people look at their subtotal at this point and assume they spend a portion of what they've already just accounted for. They might add around 20%, as illustrated in table 3.2.

Table 3.2: Lucas and Amy's estimated additional expenses per month

Additional expenses	Cost per month
Clothing	$100
Entertainment	$360
Total (incl. basics)	**$2760**

These figures are normally laughably inaccurate. First, all lenders in Australia have their own way of looking at expenditure, using a dataset from Melbourne university called the 'household expenditure measure' (HEM), which is unfortunately not publicly available. This matches household size, structure and income levels to average levels of non-housing expenditure, with higher incomes linked to higher spending. This helps lenders make an assessment of potential borrowers' financial fitness (and, therefore, their ability to service a loan).

To illustrate, here is a comparison between the HEM estimate and Lucas and Amy's actual spend. If Lucas and Amy are earning $150,000 a year before tax, according to the HEM they would spend $4000 a month. If we take out the basic expenses as listed in table 3.1, that would put clothing and entertainment at a total of $1700, or 74% of basic spending, not the $460 or 20% assumed in table 3.2. I also ask these top-down questions:

- How much did you earn for the month?
- How much do you routinely save?
- When do you dip into your savings?

Using the answers to these questions, we can begin to calculate actual expenses, as demonstrated in tables 3.3 and 3.4 (overleaf).

Table 3.3: Lucas and Amy's monthly figures – earnings less savings

Category	Value per month
Income per month (after tax)	$9300
Savings	$1800
Total spending	**$7500**

Subtracting savings from income gives us total spending, but we have to dig a little deeper if we want to get to the bottom of this couple's spending. For example, as I've set out in table 3.4, if we take away rent ($2300 in this instance) from total spending ($7500) we get the more useful theoretical spending figure of $5200. However, if we add to that the amount of money pulled out of savings to be spent on holidays, gifts and things like car registration and repairs ($800), we get the more accurate net monthly spending figure of $6000.

Table 3.4: Lucas and Amy's additional monthly figures

Expense	Value per month
Total spending (from table 3.3)	$7500
Less rent	$2300
Plus 'savings' spent on gifts, holidays, car registrations and repairs	$800
Net total spending (excluding rent)	**$6000**

Now let's compare three lots of figures:

- Lucas and Amy's estimation of their monthly spend – $2760
- the bank's monthly spending expectation – $4000
- Lucas and Amy's true monthly spend – $6000.

As you can see, these are vastly different monthly spends, with a difference of $3240 every month between what they think they spend and what they actually spend. That's $38,880 a year!

In practice, using the techniques in this book, I've found that it's very possible to put 50% of income towards rent and long-term savings (or a mortgage), which for Lucas and Amy would be around $4650 a month (rent $2300, long-term savings $2350). Compared with their current spending of $6000, that's an extra $16,200 a year in savings. This would allow the couple to spend in line with the bank estimate of $4000 a month while still putting $7800 a year ($650 a month) towards holidays and cars.

Your first thought is probably that this is unrealistic or that I've exaggerated to make a point. However, in this example, Lucas and Amy are saving 10.7% of their income ($1000 of $9300 a month – remember they're spending $800 of their total savings a month), yet the national average at time of writing is under 5%. Their income is quite typical of a couple and equates to $4292 a fortnight after tax. Their lack of savings is a result of all the little things, some of which are shown in table 3.5 (overleaf).

Add to this the less frequent purchases over the whole year, examples of which are set out in table 3.6 (overleaf). Then there are the other costs that many people forget about, such as cigarettes, alcohol and gambling (table 3.7, overleaf). It could be that just one or two – or even none – of these categories of spending apply to you, but I mention them now because they're so often overlooked.

Table 3.5: Lucas and Amy's daily, weekly and monthly purchases

Expense	Cost per month
Coffee (daily at $5 each)	$300
Soft drink for Lucas (daily at $3)	$90
Uber Eats (twice a week at $60 an order)	$480
Streaming services (three at $15 each a month)	$45
Lunch at work for Amy ($10 five days a week)	$200
Total	**$1155**

Table 3.6: sample monthly costs of less frequent purchases

Expense	Cost per month
Phones ($1000 each every two years)	$83
Christmas ($2400 a year)	$200
Holidays ($4000 a year)	$333
Haircuts ($260 for four every six weeks)	$188
Clothing ($2900 a year)	$242
Car servicing and repairs ($1200 a year)	$100
Car replacement ($30,000 every ten years)	$250
Total	**$1397**

Table 3.7: sample costs of things people tend to forget about

Expense	Cost per month
Beer ($50 case a week)	$200
Wine ($100 a fortnight)	$200
Cigarettes (ten a day at a total of $140 a week)	$560
Gambling ($1200 a year)	$100
Total	**$1160**

Apart from one client of mine, who was a professional gambler until all his accounts got shut down because he was winning too much, nobody seems to budget for gambling. Yet, it's a huge industry. It's not difficult for a gambler to go through $200 in one session. If that happens once a week that's $800 a month.

Addiction to shopping is also problematic. Think about how quick and easy it is to jump online and go through $50, $100 or $200. Things often seem like bargains because we believe they will make life simpler and easier, but before we know it we're spending hundreds of dollars a week on extra stuff. Some of that inevitably goes towards replacing things bought just the other month that either didn't last or weren't quite as good as the latest gadget. Though some items do deliver on their promise of being useful and improving our lives, others are just stuff that clutters up the house and is eventually, when we move or have a big spring clean, cleared out and thrown away.

It's no surprise, then, that Australia has very expensive rubbish. Clean Up Australia says we buy an average of 56 items of clothing a year, yet we *dump* 23 kg of clothing in landfill every year. Another problem area is electronics, which they say is our fastest growing waste category. We also spend a lot of money on supplements and vitamins, only for a lot of them to be flushed away as excess that our bodies don't need.

If we could be more discerning (using System 2 thinking) about what we buy and reduce our overall purchases, we would not only help the environment but also gain much more control over our finances. In chapter 7 I'll look at the distinct sets of variable spending and show you how to control them in a way that's easy to understand and implement. Essentially, when you spend within your limits and on your highest priority items first, it really doesn't matter what you spend money on after that. If it's an occasional flutter, glass of wine or cup of coffee, that's fine.

It just needs to fit in with the rest of your life and not become something you're doing out of habit.

Changing spending patterns

Most of us are familiar with Maslow's hierarchy of needs. Over human history, as more money has become more available to more people, our spending patterns have changed to shift us up the hierarchy of needs.

In the beginning, for most people, earning enough money to survive by covering their basic physiological needs and safety was all they could manage. Over time, however, it has become easier and easier for us to cover our basic needs. In Australia in the '70s, our basic survival needs of food and shelter used to absorb over 60% of our income, but now these take up around 50%. Interestingly the ABS puts the figure for 'basic spending' in their 2015–16 survey at 59% of total spending, but 'basic spending' covers all food, even eating out and fast food, plus all transport, including rideshare, taxis and vehicle purchase costs (including luxury vehicles). If we were to consider the low-income-household 'basic spending' as true basic spending, the same survey would show that 37% of the mean income was spent on basics, in contrast to 43% in 1975–76. With savings dropping from between 15 and 20% in the '70s to under 5% today, this means our discretionary spending has grown over the past 50 years from an average of around 20–25% of income to around 45% of income. This is used to satisfy the higher-level needs I'll discuss soon.

Before moving on, it's worth noting that while detailed data is not yet available, mortgage-holders and renters have seen significant increases in costs in recent years. The Fast and Slow System, as well as this book more generally, focuses on spending excluding mortgage and rent, since this is the part we have most control over.

Moving up the hierarchy of needs, the next stage is belonging. We spend an awful lot of money on trying to meet this need. Brand marketers are brilliant at making us feel like we need to be part of a tribe or a group, whether it's through the car that we buy, the clothes that we wear or the places where we hang out (and spend money). As we're not as worried about our survival and safety, we're free to focus on establishing our tribe or group. Additionally, we're living more and more separate lives, making a sense of belonging a much stronger unmet need than it once was.

The next level up is esteem; we want to be held in high regard. We want to feel like we have value in the world, and brand marketers play on this to try and help us get that feeling by buying their product. The top of the pyramid is self-actualisation. It's about knowing ourselves, feeling like we're in control of our lives and our destinies, and living in a way that aligns with our values.

As you might expect, when we feel like we don't belong, we experience low self-esteem or feel deeply that we're not in control of our lives, it's easy to start spending money – be that on consumer goods such as clothes or gadgets, on cosmetic treatments or programs, or on food, drugs or alcohol – to try to mask the feeling that we're missing out or that we haven't got what we want. In short, we tend to spend more money trying to cover up bad feelings than creating good ones. Think about the money spent on tattoos, cosmetic surgery and hair-loss solutions. We spend a lot of money on these things to try to make ourselves feel good. Sometimes it works, but often it doesn't. Either way, the money is gone.

What Kelly has learned over the many years of working within a spending plan is that researching a great product while saving for it, looking for alternatives and reading reviews leads to far greater satisfaction and much less buyer's remorse.

How age makes a difference

I've always found it interesting that people in their 20s think they can retire by 50 but at the same time would like to travel and 'enjoy life' while they're young. Spending lots of money on travel and fun while they're young is, of course, the exact opposite of what they'd need to do to retire by 50. Then, in their 30s and 40s, many people have families, and so most of their money goes towards childcare, education and other kid-related expenses. Suddenly, they get to their 50s and realise that they'll have to work until their 70s. This causes spending habits to change.

People in their 50s are much more likely to be thinking about and trying to plan for retirement – and, of course, wishing that they'd done more in their 20s, 30s and 40s. They realise that the money spent on *things* wasn't necessary. They try to cut back where they can, but it's honestly quite difficult to reverse the habits that were ingrained in their 20s, 30s and 40s.

By the time they're in their 70s most people have retired, and they begin to look back on their lives and reflect on what they did. Grandparents try to advise their grandkids to do things differently and better than them. If they've been good with their money, they'll have a comfortable retirement. They won't have to be worried about government pensions or benefits and they'll be able to just enjoy the time that they have with the people they love.

It's also in their 70s that people tend to realise the value of spending time with people they love, with friends and family.

They don't really remember the things that they bought. The cars that they owned might stick out in their memory, but most of the rest will be in landfill. Instead, they've got memories: holidays and travel, the places they went, the people they met, the cultures they experienced and the time they spent with those they loved along the way. The wisdom of age is likely to see people spending more of their money on what makes them happy, which I covered in chapter 2. In their 70s, or even as early as their 50s, regret also starts to seep in – a feeling that they could've done better. They could've done more. Why didn't they mend that relationship? Why didn't they pursue their goals and do what they really wanted to do? Could they have achieved more on the way? Should they have saved more? Should they have bought that property in their 20s? They could've sold it in their retirement and made a fortune!

There's also the bizarre paradox that young people seem reluctant to listen to older people, because what did they achieve in their lives? Why should they listen to someone who didn't get it right? Of course, what they don't realise is that older people know better *because* of the mistakes they made – the things they could and should have done. That's typically the advice that they want to give out – to do the things that they didn't do and avoid the things they did. By not listening to this advice, people in their 20s and 30s will probably repeat the mistakes of their elders and find themselves with the same problems and regrets in 40 or 50 years' time.

The way to break this cycle is to imagine yourself as an older person looking back on and judging your actions today with the benefit of hindsight. That's why I find goal setting such a valuable thing to do with clients. I often talk to 30-year-olds in terms of celebrating their 50th or 60th birthdays, thinking about themselves with grown-up children when they haven't even found a life partner yet. I want to help people make better decisions by imagining themselves in the future.

What I find funny is that everyone assumes they make rational, sensible decisions, considering all the information, all of the time. The truth is, until they get into their 70s, they probably don't really have the time to do that. When you're not having to go to work every day and you have more time on your hands, you're more likely to think about what you do before you do it and therefore make better decisions. When you're in your 20s and 30s, you're so busy living life, going to work, getting home and watching the latest episode or taking care of kids that you simply don't have the time to consider what you're doing before you do it. You just need to get on with it and make decisions and hope that things work out OK in the end.

This book is designed to help people get better with money but without taking away their ability to give to others, travel and have holidays. In my opinion, those sorts of spending behaviours should be a priority, because that's likely to be what's most valuable later in life.

Summary

- Understanding money starts with understanding yourself and where your money really goes, rather than assuming it all goes into bills and big stuff.
- Your first impressions of your spending are likely to be wildly inaccurate. Either look back at what you've spent in detail or use the top-down method (annual income less annual increase in savings is equal to annual spending).

- Australians are saving less and spending more on discretionary items now than they were 50 years ago.
- As we age, we're more likely to value relationships and experiences, which aligns with Dunn and Norton's *Happy Money* findings as discussed in chapter 2. The key is to imagine ourselves older and spend time learning the lessons of the elderly before we repeat their mistakes.

Chapter 4
Goal setting

In my opinion, goal setting is the highest form of System 2 thinking, where we're not just thinking rationally and logically but also taking the time to plan our future. Requiring hard, effortful thinking, it's no surprise that 80% of us never actually set ourselves any goals, while those who do rarely write down their goals where they can see them on a regular basis. That's concerning, because people who not only think about their goals but also write them down, have a game plan to achieve them and report progress to a supportive friend are around 77% more likely to achieve their goals than those who just think about them and don't write them down or tell anyone. What's clear, then, is that writing down goals is an important step if we intend to reach them.

What I've noticed in my professional practice, where I often work with couples to help them reach their financial goals, is that sitting down with our partner (if we have one) to match different types of goals is a step that we need to take. Often, there's one person in the relationship who leads financial discussions, but whenever they've tried to do the goals by themselves and I've insisted on discussing them jointly with their partner, there have always been adjustments and misunderstandings. I've also yet to find a partner walk away or zone out from a big-picture goals discussion, despite many doing so once we get down to details of monthly bills and loan interest rates.

One exception was an enthusiastic young woman who was only two months into a relationship. I asked her what she wanted from this or a future relationship, such as kids or marriage. She went straight home and shared the outcomes with her boyfriend, who promptly signed up for the whole lot! They came back to see me six months later with very few changes to the young woman's original long-term plan and a commitment to work on it together.

This chapter is going to help you break down and put in place goals to help you in the future.

Goal setting, fast and slow

What I often find when talking with people about their goals is how often those goals compete with or contradict one another. For example, it's quite common to meet a young person who wants to get into the housing market, and their goal might be to buy an apartment because that's what they want to live in and that's what they can afford; however, they might also be planning to start a family soon, and so they soon won't fit comfortably into the apartment they plan to buy.

This is classic System 1 thinking: having an idea about a goal and a gut feeling that it's the right thing to do without taking the time to engage System 2 thinking. In this instance, engaging System 2 thinking would mean thinking clearly about what it means to buy property, live in a space, and start a family and have children in that space.

Instead, despite the cost of buying and selling property in Australia being around 7% of the purchase price, people with a young family or plans to start one often buy an apartment, townhouse or terrace that's big enough for them now but has no scope to increase in size when the kids get bigger, realising their mistake only much later.

To resolve these problems and anticipate future changes, I've found it's best to think much longer term and ask people to imagine themselves in the near future (one or two years away), then in the predictable next three to ten years, and then finally in their ideal long-term future (11 to 30 years out). Then we look at different, interconnected areas of their lives across these three time periods.

Since housing is our biggest cost, we have to think about the factors impacting housing before looking at where to live and what to live in. Investments are an important consideration for our long-term financial wellbeing and are often ignored until it's too late. Thinking about our careers and when we might like to be able to retire is important, as the more time people spend in jobs they don't like, the more important it is to save for a better future without their horrible job. Holidays are usually an important focus for most Australians, whether they're local camping trips or round-the-world career breaks. Health is important to consider over the long term, too, as it impacts our spending on better foods and sporting activities. Lastly, we need to think about other big things, such as new cars, weddings, important anniversaries and milestone birthdays. I always enjoy including kids' 18th and 21st birthdays in the 11- to 30-year goals for people thinking about starting a family in the next couple of years!

Table 4.1 is a template for goal setting (a version of which is also available on the Golden Eggs web app). A completed version is featured in chapter 11.

Table 4.1: goal setting template

Goal area	1–2 years	3–10 years	11–30 years
Relationship/ family/schooling			
Where and what to live in			
Investments			
Career			
Holidays			
Health			
Celebrations, cars and other big things			

Though we don't have full control over things like having kids, the better aligned a couple is on what they want in each area, the better they will anticipate and work towards a great shared future. Thinking about the future in this way and articulating it to one another, or simply writing it down, is a great way to not only look forward to a great life but also remind yourselves that spending all your money today could mean missing out tomorrow.

What's your why?

Simon Sinek put it brilliantly in *Start With Why* when he wrote, 'The WHY provides the context for everything else'. When it comes to money, if you're not working towards any goals, if you don't have anything you're saving up or preventing overspending for, then why not spend all your money right now? That's the way most of us spend money. We'll have an intuition or thought that we want something, we'll see it and, if we have the money, we'll buy it. The only way to stop this is by articulating some really good reasons for delaying gratification and instead spending in another way later.

We can only earn a finite amount of money within our lifetimes, and we can only spend a finite amount of money within our lifetimes. Some people have a goal to leave something behind for the kids, for the family, for the next generation. That's a great goal, but it means they need to not spend all their money while they're alive, which will take some careful planning.

Many of us have some shorter-term goals. Perhaps we want to take a holiday, get a new car or buy a house. These are things that we know we need to save up for, which means we need to spend less now so that we may spend that money on those other things later. But, of course, the whole lending industry is designed around letting us have those things now and paying for them later. So instead of saving up and then buying, we buy now and then spend the next several years paying them off. Of course, we know that's a lot more expensive in the long run, but it's a way of achieving our goals. It's just not a very good one.

When we have a strong enough reason to do something else with our money, perhaps something in the future, it becomes much easier to restrain ourselves in the present and take action that will help us get where we want to go. That's why goal setting is so important, but for now, we're going to focus on two goals that motivate a lot of people.

Why holidays are so important

One of the most common reasons for delaying spending now is to save up for a holiday or big trip. The great news is that psychologists tell us experiences are more valuable in terms of our happiness and building long-term memories than things – and holidays set us up for experiences.

In *Happy Money*, which I first mentioned in chapter 2, Dunn and Norton provide great insight into the importance of holidays to our happiness. As they explain, we get pleasure from holidays in three distinct time frames. The first is the planning phase. It's exciting and fun and rewarding to plan for a holiday. It gets us excited about the future and makes us happy. The second is when we're actually on the holiday, experiencing the trip. This is what we were looking forward to in the previous phase, but now we're enjoying being on the beach, spending time with our friends and doing all sorts of fun, relaxing and exciting things. The third time frame is after the experience itself has passed, and we're remembering and reminiscing about the holiday that we've just been on.

Once again, it's interesting to think about these three happiness time frames alongside *Thinking, Fast and Slow*, in which Kahneman talks about the distinction between two types of memory. There's the 'remembering self', which remembers past events but has a bias towards extremes, looking favourably upon some things and less favourably upon others. There's also the 'experiencing self', which is what you're experiencing at the time. The strange thing is that we often forget how we felt during the experiences or put less weight on our feelings at the time when we're remembering them later. We tend to look back through rose-tinted glasses.

It's bizarre, but even if we have a terrible holiday filled with horrible experiences – be that an awful hotel, terrible weather or anything else that could go wrong going wrong – we'll still derive pleasure from telling and remembering those stories. This is because we love human interaction. It's what makes us enjoy life. If we've got a great story to tell, the telling is enjoyable, even if we look back and laugh at our own misfortune. The funny thing is that the more we tell the story of what a terrible holiday we had, the more we enjoy the fact that we took that terrible holiday.

Another interesting holiday phenomenon relates closely to what I discussed towards the end of chapter 3. As we get older and look back on decades of our lives, things like holidays stand out in our memories and make us feel we had rich and full lives. We tend to forget the work-week routine and instead remember the trips we took, the places we went and all the people we spent time with. We can essentially think about holidays as investments in our memory banks that will help us enjoy our later years, especially when we're unable to do the things we dreamt of doing when we were younger.

Where money and goal setting fits into all of this is that when we save up for a holiday in a special bank account that we label 'Holiday', it encourages us to look forward to, get excited about and plan for that trip. It also means that when we're actually on the holiday, we've got the money to do what we want to do because we planned for it. Importantly, when it's all over and we're reminiscing about the time we had, we won't have that sick feeling in our guts, that worry about how we're going to pay a credit card bill or personal loan that we took out to take the holiday.

In contrast, if we don't save for the holiday, it's just a thought – *I want to go on holiday*. We probably don't have the money, so we mightn't start planning or thinking too much beyond that vague want, and we miss out on all that excitement we'd experience if we were saving to reach our goal. Eventually, we give in and book after taking out a personal loan, or we put it on a credit card. Now we're looking forward to the holiday because it's happening! However, while we're away, we're already feeling guilty about the debt we're running up. We're more likely to say 'no' to things that we would've enjoyed. These things that would make the holiday more enjoyable and memorable don't happen because we're worried about how big the credit card bill will be or how quickly the personal loan will run out. Then, when we come back at the end of the holiday, every single time we make a payment we' get more and more annoyed about taking the holiday in the first place. This detracts from the enjoyment that we get. We may have spent the same amount of money – though with interest it would probably be a bit more – but we won't get the same amount of pleasure from the holiday that we could have if we'd we saved up for it.

It's important to remember that money is a tool to help us achieve our goals, like enjoying great holidays, and make our lives better. It's not the end goal.

When I retire...

Retirement seems so far away when we're in our 20s that many of us are convinced we'll have everything sorted out by the time we reach 50. I remember feeling the same way when I was in my 20s. My wife and I even did a goal setting exercise together in which we envisioned that exact conclusion! However, the problem is that unless we take concrete steps to make that plan a reality, time tends to slip away from us. Life gets busy, we start families, our careers take off, and before we know it another decade has gone by and we're already turning 40, thinking it would be great to retire by 60.

This is why it's so important to use System 2 thinking to set concrete goals and come up with a plan to achieve them. If we don't, autopilot will take over, and we'll keep spending too much money on things like coffee, takeaway and credit-funded holidays without making any real progress towards our retirement goals. Unfortunately, the average Australian retires at 67, and they usually have only a modest amount of money in superannuation. This means that they'll likely have to live on the Age Pension for a couple of decades, if they're lucky. The Age Pension in Australia is relatively generous compared with those of other countries, but it still only provides a couple with around $41,700 a year ($1604 a fortnight).

During their working lives, the average couple earns over $140,000 a year before tax, but they save less than 5% of their income. When the pandemic hit and many of us couldn't go out and spend money, the savings rate briefly shot up to 20% and then settled at around 10% to 12% until things opened up again. However, financial commentators suggest saving at least 20% of our income if we want to retire comfortably; for example, you may have heard of the 50:30:20 rule, proposed by Elizabeth Warren and Amelia Warren Tyagi in *All Your Worth*, which suggests spending 50% of our income on needs, spending 30% on wants and putting 20% into savings.

The maths is simple: if we can live on 80% of our income during our working lives, we can accumulate enough assets to continue living on 80% of our pre-retirement income when we retire. In most cases, we only need to live on about 50% to 60% of our pre-retirement income, since many of us put about 20% to 30% of our income towards a home or rent, and hopefully can we stop renting, buy a place and pay off the mortgage by the time we retire. According to the Australian government's MoneySmart website, a comfortable retirement for a couple requires just under $71,000 a year, which is over 50% more than the Age Pension. This means that though the Age Pension is not generous enough to support a comfortable lifestyle, if we haven't been putting money aside, that's what we'll have to live on.

When I ask people in their 20s when they want to retire, I like to follow up with another question: 'What do you want to *do* when you retire?' Most people don't want to just sit on the couch all day and do nothing. Many of us want to continue to contribute to society, and studies show that people live longer when they feel they have a purpose in life. The clearer we get on what we'd like to do in retirement, the easier it is to visualise our future and focus on what we really want out of life. For some people, it could be volunteering or working for a charity. It might be visiting family and friends or pursuing hobbies. Many people say they want to travel, but travel can be exhausting, and we all need breaks to rest and recuperate.

Anthony and Tonie are two of the happiest people in their 60s that I know. They're working two days a week, which they love. They also love their five-day weekends, which is when they get to spend time with their grandkids and friends, relax playing golf and enjoy other hobbies. Then they go back to work for two days, and those two days keep them motivated and make them feel like they're still contributing. Think about how fantastic a five-day weekend would be! If you fully retire and stop working, then you don't get weekends anymore – every day just blends into the next.

The happiest retirees are those who get to pursue their hobbies and spend a lot of time with friends and family members. That's because as we get older we realise that our relationships are what's most important to us. It's not collecting things or having the shiniest new possessions that makes us happy; it's connecting with friends and family, and enjoying life.

The clearer you get on what you'd like to do to enjoy your life when you retire, the easier it is to imagine or envisage a way to do some of those activities before you get to retirement. Of course, the most important element is to make sure that you're planning for retirement, so it doesn't just happen by accident or because the government says so.

As I mentioned a moment ago, it's generally thought that a comfortable retirement can be achieved by saving, at minimum, about 20% of your total income. The big question, then, is how do you save 20% of your income? The answer is simple, but it's not easy.

The first step is to set a savings goal. That means deciding on a specific amount or percentage of your income that you want to save each month or year. It's important to make this goal realistic and achievable so you can stick to it.

The next step is to create a spending plan that allows you to live on 80% of your income. This means tracking your expenses and cutting back on things that are not essential. It might mean making some sacrifices in the short term, but it will be worth it in the long run. There are plenty of budgeting tools available online, or you can create your own spreadsheet to help you keep track of your spending, but the rest of this book contains a great process – the Fast and Slow System – for consistently sticking to whatever budget you set.

Another way to save more money is to increase your income. This might mean asking for a raise at work, taking on a side hustle or starting your own business. Obviously, quitting the day job to start your own business comes with a greater risk of failure and a likely drop in income in the short term, but in my opinion there's greater upside potential in the long run. Either way, the more money you earn, the more you can save.

It's also important to have a plan for your savings. That means investing your money in assets that will grow over time. This might include stocks, bonds or property. It's important to do your research and seek advice from a financial professional before making any investment decisions. I am biased towards property, as revealed in my previous book *Getting Your Money $hit Together*.

Finally, it's important to stay motivated and on track. It's easy to be distracted by short-term pleasures and forget about your long-term goals. That's why it's important to revisit your goals regularly and remind yourself why you're saving. Celebrate your successes along the way and stay focused on the end goal.

In conclusion, saving for retirement isn't easy, but it's essential if you want to have a comfortable and fulfilling life in your later years. By setting realistic goals, creating a spending plan, increasing your income, investing wisely and staying motivated, you can achieve financial security and the freedom to enjoy your retirement to the fullest.

Summary

- Setting goals is the first step to having some semblance of control over your life.
- Setting goals can help you to get on the right path and start to prioritise your decisions, especially about money.

- Knowing your own goals for the short, medium and long term can give you greater clarity and highlight obvious problems with competing goals.
- Knowing why you're doing what you're doing can be a powerful motivating force.
- Holidays are great experiences to build happiness, which comes as much from looking forward to the holiday and reminiscing about it afterwards as from the holiday itself.
- Retirement doesn't have to mean giving up work completely. You can retain your purpose and get more out of life by continuing to work in some capacity. Planning for the retirement you want is important.

Chapter 5

Where are you now?

Before we look at why we are where we are, it's important to understand where we are. A great exercise for this, proposed by Vicki Robin in *Your Money or Your Life*, is to estimate how much we've earned so far in life, either as an individual or as a couple, and then compare that to current net assets.

Let's use Josh as an example. Josh took his first full-time job when he was age 20, earning around $45,000 per year. Now, at 30, he earns $100,000 a year. These are gross figures before tax, so we need to take the tax off and estimate how much he's been earning for all the years in between, as set out in table 5.1 (overleaf).

As we can see, Josh's total income for the last ten years is around $600,000. Next, we look at his net asset position. Josh's net asset position equals his savings, real estate, shares and any other saleable assets that could be used towards his future, minus any associated debt.

As shown in table 5.2 (overleaf), Josh has a net asset position of $80,000. Now we simply divide Josh's net asset position ($80,000) by his total income over his working life ($600,000) to work out that Josh has held onto 13% of his income.

Table 5.1: total income over ten years

Age	Salary	Net (after tax)
21	$45,000	$38,874
22	$50,000	$42,799
23	$55,000	$46,724
24	$65,000	$54,574
25	$70,000	$58,499
26	$75,000	$62,424
27	$80,000	$66,349
28	$90,000	$74,199
29	$95,000	$78,124
30	$100,000	$82,049
Total		**$604,615**

Table 5.2: net asset position

Savings	$100,000
Car loan	$20,000
Net assets	**$80,000**

My recommended savings rate, on top of saving up for other things like cars and holidays, is 20%. Had Josh managed to save 20% of his income over that time frame, he would instead be sitting on net assets of $120,000 (plus interest). We also need to account for the fact that Josh lived at home with his parents and didn't pay rent or bills for the first five years of his working life, meaning he could easily have saved half his income during that time. That would've given him an additional $45,000 of savings, pushing him up to about $165,000 in net assets.

More importantly, had Josh used the first five years of ideal savings to buy himself a property, he would be paying a mortgage instead of rent. If he got lucky with the property market, he could've had about five years growth. This could easily have added $100,000 to his net asset position. It's easy to see that Josh has fallen behind where he could've been had he been more careful with his money and started investing sooner. By around the age of 40, the gap can be huge when we consider the gains that could've been made from investing over an additional ten years.

Do your own calculations now, being honest with yourself about where you are compared to where you could be, but don't beat yourself up. After all, 67% of Australians need to live on a full or partial Age Pension when they retire, but it's much better to find out you've got a problem now and take steps to fix it than be surprised at age 67.

The other consideration is the impact of long-term compounding growth of investments. This can be projected using MoneySmart's compound interest calculator, but here's a simple example of what's possible. Investing just $100 per month (that's $1200 a year every year) from the age of 20 into a standard index fund growing by 7% a year would net $379,259 by age 65. However, waiting ten years and starting at 30 more than halves the total to only $180,105. In other words, the sooner we stop spending all our hard-earned money and start saving and investing, the better off we'll be in the long term.

Where is your money going?

Having identified where you stand financially, the next step is to look at your spending habits and find out where your money is going. While many experts recommend looking back at just the last month, this approach may not give an accurate picture due to bills that come quarterly or yearly. Then there's higher-spend periods like holidays and Christmas, which add to the annual spend but not the monthly spend. Therefore, it's crucial to look at actual spending over a full year to gain a clear understanding of your financial situation.

You can begin by using a spend-tracking app to sort your spending into different categories (this is another function available in the Golden Eggs web app). Many banks offer this feature, allowing customers to look back at up to a year's worth of spending. Alternatively, you can take a more manual approach, going through each bill (for electricity, gas, phone and so on) and adding up your annual spending. You can also estimate variable expenses, such as entertainment and dining out, and add those in as well.

To ensure the accuracy of your calculations, you need to reconcile your spending with your income and savings. You can do this by subtracting your increase in long-term savings from your total income for the year. This method helps you focus on saving in ways that will benefit you in the long run, rather than helping you reach only your short-term goals, such as a holiday or a new car. If you have reduced your personal loans or credit card debt during the year, that is still considered an increase in net position. On the other hand, if you have taken out new loans or increased your credit card debt, you'll need to add that back into your total spending.

Whether using a manual spreadsheet, a planning tool (such as the Golden Eggs web app) or a spend-tracking app, always do a top-down sense check. Table 5.3 shows an example.

Table 5.3: top-down sense-check

Category	Value over the year
Total net income (after tax and HECS*)	$85,000
Increase in long-term savings	$7000
Personal loan repayments	$1500
Total saving	**$8500**
Percentage of income saved	**10%**

*A full-time employee on close to $100,000 a year would typically have around $540 a month deducted from gross pay for HECS (6.5%).

As I've mentioned before, the average Australian spends 95% of their income and saves only 5%, which is not sufficient to secure their financial future. Therefore, it's crucial to understand your spending habits and make changes to increase your savings and investments if you'd like to experience a comfortable retirement and spend in a way that's consistent with your goals.

Making excuses

When we complete that exercise, it's very easy to make excuses for what we've been doing and how we've been going. Most of us will typically try to justify the position we're in and explain that it's unrepresentative of our usual behaviour.

I've had many of these conversations with people over the years, and they typically go along these lines:

> I know! When we remove the extra furniture that we bought last month, then our spending is actually a lot lower than that.
>
> No, we spent a bit more in the last few months because we had family coming to visit and so we went out more.
>
> We were on holiday during that period, so we spent more than usual.
>
> That was when the car rego and insurance was due, and we had to pay extra to get repairs done.
>
> Those few months include Christmas, so obviously that doesn't happen all the time.
>
> That was before we started taking a lunch to work, which we know has saved us like $50 a week.

The reason we do both of these exercises together is because it makes it easy to see the difference between how much of our money we think we're spending and how much we're actually spending. Any excuses we then make up for why our actual spending is so high are also obviously System 1 thinking at play. We know that Christmas is going to come around every year. We know the car is going to need registering every year and there'll be some repairs. We know that we're going to have family coming to visit from time to time. All these are things that we could've anticipated using System 2 thinking, budgeted for and had a spending plan in place for – and that's what we're going to talk about in chapter 7.

Kanika and Diya: Saving for the World Cup

When I first met Kanika and Diya, they had a very small amount of savings relative to their income. When we looked back at what they had been spending their money on, they immediately focused on the big things, such as the trip back to India that they did every year, the gifts they bought for their nieces and nephews at Christmas, the live concerts they went to, the rent that they had to pay and the cost of running a car.

The interesting thing is that when we looked at the things they wanted to do, which included saving up to go to the FIFA World Cup in a couple of years' time, it was easy to still find enough funds for concerts, Christmas, going back to India and making sure the rent was covered. It just meant that there was less money available week to week. In fact, when we started adding up all the small things they did on a regular basis, the biggest cost seemed to be alcohol, cigarettes and takeaways.

It seems so obvious in hindsight that if there was always alcohol in the house, Kanika and Diya were likely to have a drink every evening. It was also likely that if they didn't plan their spending and organise their meals, they would feel tired and order takeaway. Of course, cigarettes were going to be hard to cut out of the budget. As we know, nicotine is highly addictive, so smokers' bodies will tell them that they need more cigarettes, and they can find themselves going to buy more cigarettes without really realising until they break that pattern. Years later, having helped Kanika and Diya to implement the Fast and Slow System that we'll go through in part II, it was lovely to get a message from Kanika that she had finally stopped smoking and couldn't believe how much extra money was now available.

No matter where you think you're spending your money or what your priorities are, in practice people are very likely to succumb to very short-term temptations. If you do that repeatedly over a long period of time, you'll end up spending more than you think you do. Most of your focus when ascertaining where you are now financially – and why – should be on small, regular, fast spending.

Summary

- Before looking to make changes, it's important to understand how much of your money you've been able to hang onto and what happened to the rest.
- Working out your lifetime net income and comparing it to your net asset position is a good wake-up call on the results of your past behaviour if your aim is to save 20% of net income, or 50% if living rent-free.
- Conduct a thorough review of your spending habits and focus on the cumulative effect of the small things, rather than just the big items of expenditure.
- Avoid making quick excuses for current shortfalls. This only serves to delay making changes.
- Saving for multiple goals simultaneously is perfectly possible and will help with cutting back on the small things.

Chapter 6

Having a budget versus sticking to it

In 2018, a ubank study of 1021 Australians found that 86% don't know how much they spend every month, and only 28% use some kind of tool to manage their money. A similar US study by Intuit in 2020 found that 65% of Americans have no idea how much they spent the previous month, with Gen Z and Millennials at over 80%. A more recent study by ubank found that 65% of Australians have some kind of a budget. For those who *do* have a budget, many find it difficult to stick to for more than a few months at a time due to variable income or expenses. It's a common problem.

In my experience, many people's idea of a budget is more of a rule of thumb. Maybe they aim to save a certain amount each month or ensure their credit card bill doesn't exceed a certain amount. Others simply don't like the idea of working to a budget, or what we prefer to call a 'spending plan.'

I remember being at a party and telling someone what I do for a living. When I mentioned the word 'budget', he immediately responded, 'I don't like working to a budget. I like to enjoy my life.' I asked him how many helicopters he'd bought that year, to which he replied, 'What?' I then asked if he'd bought any fancy cars or taken any exotic vacations. He said he hadn't because he couldn't afford it. So, I pointed out that he did, in fact, have a budget; he'd just set it to 100% of his income!

Now, there's nothing inherently wrong with setting your budget to 100% of your income – if your plan is to work until you die, or live on the Age Pension in retirement. If that's not your plan, then it's important to consider the long-term consequences of not working out and sticking to a more useful spending plan.

Interestingly, in my experience, having a budget and not sticking to it is just as bad as not having a budget at all. That's why the focus of this book is on figuring out how to stick to a spending plan, regardless of whether you have one written down. It's all about mimicking the behaviour of someone who *does* stick to a budget and making small changes to your spending habits to help you get there.

My preferred approach, which my wife and I have been using for over 20 years and clients of ours have been using for over a decade, is to tie in a spending plan with the way your banking is managed.

Are you set up to spend fast?

'I can resist anything except temptation' is a famous line from Oscar Wilde's play *Lady Windermere's Fan*, and ain't it the truth!

In Australia, where most people use electronic forms of payment and don't physically handle cash as much, it can be easy to lose track of how much money you're spending. As I covered in chapter 3, the more money you have access to, the more likely you are to spend it, and we call this being 'set up to spend fast'. No matter how hard you try to save and concentrate on your financial goals, sooner or later a lapse in concentration in the face of temptation will lead you back to your old habits of spending money that's easily accessible.

It's important to remember that temptation is everywhere. Knowing how you access your own money will make it easier to understand your past errors and then plan to fix them.

Problem banking structures

Many of us set up our bank account structure when we're teenagers and never change the way we do things. Or, if we do, we repeat the same mistakes that we made when we opened our first everyday transaction account for our very first job, giving ourselves debit card access to all our pay. Most people do this, but it's a real problem in my opinion! Before we explore stronger set-ups in part II of this book, here are some problem structures and why they're very unlikely to work for normal people.

One everyday account, one savings account and one credit card

The problem with this system is the credit card, which can trap people in a cycle of using it for everything, waiting for their pay to come in, paying off the credit card and then having to live on the credit card again the next month because they don't have any money left. Psychologically, the credit card gives full control of spending to System 1 thinking. If someone feels like they need something, they can just tap their credit card and get it instantly. Even if they try to concentrate and build up the money in their savings account, it's very likely that it will get drawn down to clear a credit card bill when they spend more than they should in any given month.

One everyday account and one savings account

While this structure is better than having a credit card, it's still open to two major problems. The first is what happens when someone runs out of money in their everyday account and has a bill due: it's very easy to dip into savings to pay that bill. The second problem is that the savings themselves tend to get spent, whether it's on a holiday, a car or something else. By the end of the year, someone could have done well, spending only 50% to 80% of their income month to month and 'saving' the rest, but then they blow most of those savings on a holiday. This could easily put them at having spent 95% of their yearly income.

One everyday account and two savings accounts

This is an improvement on the previous scenario because with this approach someone can separate their savings into savings for the future and savings to spend on things such as holidays and cars. Scott Pape calls this second category a 'splurge' account in *The Barefoot Investor*. However, people who do this are still stuck with the biggest problem of a single everyday account: their salary lands there and they can access all of it, and bills are paid from the same account. Bills tend to come monthly, quarterly and yearly, not just weekly, fortnightly or monthly with their pay cycle, so they tend to dip into one of their savings accounts when they're inevitably caught out by an overspend.

Two savings accounts and two transaction accounts

This is another improvement. It moves away from the idea of one everyday account and allows someone to have their salary deposited into one transaction account and use that account to cover bills while using their second transaction account for everyday spending. It's a great way to smooth out bills and take them away from daily spending while still benefiting from multiple savings accounts. The typical problem here is the pay cycle, which most people tend to match their budgets to. Those paid weekly (or even more frequently) tend to spend too much on small stuff and then dip into savings for big-ticket items. Those paid monthly tend to buy bigger things at the start of the month and have to dip into savings in the fourth or dreaded fifth week of the month.

The 'buckets' approach

One well-known approach to banking, which was popularised by Scott Pape in *The Barefoot Investor*, recommends doing all your banking with a single low-cost bank and separating money into four 'buckets': an everyday account (joint if partnered), a safety net account (Pape calls this a 'Mojo bucket'), a 'splurge' account and a savings/investment account. The aim is to distribute your income by percentages across these four accounts, with the assumption being that budgeting is done monthly or fortnightly to match your pay cycle.

I have a few issues with this approach. First, you're relying on the same everyday account for both deposits and expenses. This makes it difficult to adjust for pay rises and variable incomes. It also requires users to actively change the amounts allocated to other accounts, which many people don't do consistently. For example, if you receive a pay rise or some additional income, the system doesn't automatically adjust the amounts transferred to other accounts, which means it's easy to end up spending the extra income instead of allocating it properly.

It also mixes bills with everyday spending, which I've mentioned leads to people dipping into savings when bigger bills come through. There's also the problem of both in a couple spending from the same account. This might work for couples if both of you are frugal, but for others (my wife and I included) it can lead to accidental overspending and disagreements over who is responsible for the financial shortfall. For instance, one might say, 'You went to the pub with your friends, and that's why we're over budget', while the other might counter, 'But you bought a new handbag and shoes, and that's what put us over'.

Any budgeting system in which you give yourself access to what is left of your income will cause you problems over the long term, especially if you're someone with variable income or income that is likely to increase over time. Remember, humans are basically lazy and don't want to engage System 2 by doing a new budget just because they get a pay rise, a bonus or something. Instead, you're likely to use your gut feel and impulses to spend it as you go or blow it on one big item. Worse still, you simply won't change the amount that you're saving. You fixed the amount that you're saving and then, as your income grows, you just spend the extra because you can access it.

Doing everything with one bank also doesn't address the accessibility concern highlighted in chapter 3. If you check your banking app when you don't have enough in one of your spending accounts, it's too easy to dip into the Mojo or other accounts without properly engaging System 2 thinking.

Finally, though automating savings can certainly be helpful in terms of creating a consistent savings plan, it may not address the underlying psychological and behavioural issues that lead to overspending in the first place. It also encourages us, as lazy humans, to not bother increasing our savings amount as incomes rise or bonuses come in, which means we default to higher spending.

One size doesn't fit all

My goal with this book is to focus less on *where* your money is going and instead attack the root causes of *how* your money is disappearing. Without addressing those root causes, you may find yourself constantly struggling to stick to your priorities. That will ultimately mean you stop making progress towards your financial goals.

Overall, it's important to take a holistic approach to managing your finances that addresses both the practical and psychological aspects of your relationship with money. Addressing these issues is essential for creating a more effective and sustainable money management system. Additionally, if you're in a relationship, finding a solution that works for both people without completely changing the psychology of one is also important. As I mentioned in chapter 2, this has had a huge effect on my life personally.

As you can see, while automating savings and consciously choosing spending priorities are common approaches to budgeting and saving, they may not be the most effective long-term solutions for everyone. In fact, these measures may be substandard to the Fast and Slow System I propose in the next part this book.

Summary

- Having a budget already puts you ahead of most people, but sticking to it is much harder and most people are set up to fail.
- Many common bank account structures encourage fast spending.

- More bank accounts, or 'buckets', do lead to better outcomes, but even some of the most popular of these are still flawed and lead to reduced savings.
- One size doesn't fit all, and the next chapters will show you exactly how to tap into your psychology, rather than expecting yourself or your partner to change.

PART II

RESTRUCTURING THE FLOW OF MONEY

Chapter 7

The Fast and Slow System

The Fast and Slow System is designed to restrict our access to our money, especially our income, when we're not really thinking. It's a modern take on the concept of getting paid in cash, hiding all the money at home and walking back out the door with only enough cash for the day. That system worked for centuries.

The interim system, which served many people well through the '80s and '90s, was to withdraw cash instead of using cards. Things have been changing, however, and now COVID-19 has virtually killed off cash in Australia, meaning digital payment – not cash – is king. Even if you want to revert to the old way of using cash, the difficulties mount quickly. For example, if you opt for cash alone, you'll be cut off from making any purchases online. Plus, the reduction in the number of ATMs makes cash hard to access, particularly if you want to avoid paying fees.

So, how do we get the same benefits of cash in a modern, cashless world? Part of the answer lies in what I call 'double banking', and the other part lies in access and visibility. The aim is to introduce friction into our transactions and take advantage of our own laziness.

Double banking

What if, instead of fixing our savings amount each pay, we fix our variable spending? Using this approach, which is different to most people's, we can accurately predict the total of all our variable spending for an entire year. Imagine that without looking at any bank transactions we could know precisely how much discretionary spending we've had for the whole of last year and what it will be for the whole of this year. Though we might have no clue what it was all spent on, it doesn't really matter; the money was in the spending plan, and it's gone now.

This is achieved by using an *entirely different bank* for spending than what is used for income and bills. Essentially:

Bank A for income bills and saving + Bank B for spending
= double banking

Fixed spending is harder to predict due to fluctuations in bills and inflation, but the variability across the year is much lower than most people's variable spending across a month. The focus of this system, therefore, is to fix the variable spending for the year, leaving more for bills and savings.

Incomes can also vary across the year, with hours worked, bonuses, pay rises, overtime, job changes and so on coming into effect. Separating income from discretionary spending, which is what double banking does, stops us accidentally overspending when we earn more.

Credit and debit cards are highly successful in getting us to spend our money because they reduce friction. Friction in transactions is anything that slows us down when we're making a purchase – anything that makes us think. If we feel like we want something and we can just tap a card (often without even looking), there's virtually no friction. Having to go back home and fetch money (which is what our forebears had to do) or look at our budget and decide whether it's something that we really want to purchase or not introduces friction. Our goal is to re-introduce friction like this to slow down our spending. The easiest way of doing this is to completely change how we view the bank accounts that we use.

The principles of this system are as follows:

1. Separate discretionary spending from bills.
2. Radically change the flow of money.
3. Remove all instant access to the bank where we're paid.
4. Use a different bank account with a different bank for spending.

The bank set-up that forms part of the Fast and Slow System comprises three accounts for spending:

1. a transaction account with Bank A, just for bills, where all your pay is deposited
2. a transaction account (each, if in a partnership) with Bank B for weekly spending
3. a savings account with Bank B for fun stuff (sometimes each, if in a partnership, depending on money personalities).

Bills account

Once we separate bills from discretionary spending, money starts to make sense again and we can forget about pay cycles. Bills tend to come monthly, quarterly and yearly. They are predictable over a year, with slight variations, but not over a pay cycle. Keeping a buffer of three months' worth of bills in the bills account and having all our pay land there makes it easier to automate everything and stop worrying. It also now means that we get to choose when to transfer spending money, since sticking to a pay cycle also makes no sense.

Weekly spending account

The flow of money *must* move away from the traditional model of pay landing in the account used for daily spending. This is why we set up a different bank account for weekly spending (one *each* if in a partnership). Once we separate discretionary spending from bills and income, we can be confident that money in the spending account is OK to spend. We can also now receive funds in a timeframe that makes sense.

We all have a weekly routine, which typically includes grocery shopping (more on that in a moment), coffee, lunch and other regular habits. Matching transfers from the account we get paid into (the bills account) to our habits makes it easier to stick to our plan. Transfers for spending need to happen weekly. It doesn't matter if we're paid weekly, fortnightly or monthly, our routine follows a weekly cycle, so that's when we want to receive spending money.

Most people class groceries as a bill, as Kelly and I used to. The problem was, whenever I went shopping, as a tight arse, it was at Aldi or similar and most of what was purchased was on special; whenever Kelly shopped, however, it was at a nicer supermarket, selecting all branded goods in the preferred-size packs with no regard to specials. When we set the spending plan, we normally add the grocery budget to the weekly spend of the person who normally does the shopping. If the responsibility for groceries switches between the two of you, or you shop together, I suggest going by personality, which I'll cover in more detail in chapter 8. Within a few weeks of taking control of groceries as part of her discretionary spending, Kelly was shopping at Aldi and looking for specials so she had more money to spend on herself.

One of the reasons the Fast and Slow System is so successful is that you no longer have instant access to the account you're paid into. To achieve this, you need to remove all access to that bank from your phone and your wallet. No cards, no digital wallet on your phone or watch and no app on your phone, either. Having coached lots of people into this, I know this scaring you already, but all you need to do now to be able to access your money is open another bank account with a different bank, your 'spending bank'. I'll go into this in more detail in chapter 11.

Your spending bank is the one that you're going to do all your discretionary spending from. This includes paying for groceries, work lunches, coffees, entertainment, meals out, gifts, gadgets, clothes – all the things you want more of but understand you need to limit your spending on.

If you're in a couple, it's normally best to have one weekly spending account each. This allows each individual to have complete control and autonomy over what they spend and how.

Building on the discussion in chapter 3 on access, no matter when you're paid, I've found that if you get a fixed amount every week it's much easier to stick to the plan. Importantly if you run out of money, knowing there's more landing in a few days makes it much easier to manage than having to wait half a month, or half a fortnight.

Once we have our weekly budget and spend the bulk of it on groceries, whatever's left is fine to spend on coffee, lunches, takeaways, brunch on the weekend – whatever we feel like. In my first book, *Getting Your Money $hit Together*, I explain how my wife suggested cutting back on the weekly routine of pizza at home so that she could get her nails done each week. Getting her nails done made her feel good about herself, and really, it took me ten minutes to make spaghetti bolognaise, while waiting for pizza takes closer to 30 minutes.

Fun account(s)

With basic bills and everyday spending separated, our lives are automatically going to be easier. However, if all we do is pay bills and live week to week, we'll struggle with the bigger events like birthdays and Christmas, needing to buy clothes or replace the washing machine and other irregular purchases. For that, we need a savings account where we put a lump of money every month. We can call this our 'fun' or 'splurge' account.

What we call it doesn't matter, but the timing of deposits does. I've found the best approach is to pay yourself an allowance into this account on the first of the month, no matter when you're paid. This is based on the way we recall events. I've noticed that people find it easier to think of birthdays, weekends away and concerts when they use a calendar month as a framework, as compared to using a pay cycle, which could fall fortnightly or in the middle of the month. Knowing that June has no birthdays or events, for example, gives us permission to splurge on other things, while knowing that May includes Mother's Day reminds us to set aside funds for that. It's also easier to think of the upcoming months. For example, spending all the monthly money in October and November might not be the best idea, knowing that Christmas is coming. It might instead be a great idea to start the Christmas shopping early when spending money arrives on 1 October.

Some couples choose to have a fun account each, while some only have one between the two of them. As is often the case, this depends on individual money personalities, which we'll dive into in chapter 8.

With bills, weekly spending and fun now sorted, everything else must be savings, but it's important to understand what we're saving for.

Goal saving

The biggest mistake many of us make with our savings is having only one bank account where we direct all the money we want to save. The problem with having only one savings account is that we either focus purely on our future (long-term saving), denying ourselves holidays and other big-ticket items, or we end up spending all our savings on short-term saving goals and never keep anything for the long run.

We are better at saving for multiple things at a time when they're separated out and labelled accordingly. Back in chapter 4, we set out a whole load of different goals for ourselves. If any of those goals require money, set up accounts for them now. A goal account that most of us have is for holidays, but you might also need one for a wedding, a car, Christmas or something else that's important to you.

Most banks offer goal saving accounts, and these typically pay a higher rate of interest if we keep depositing money. This is a good feature that we want to take advantage of. It's also easier to deny ourselves the little luxuries week to week if we know that we're working towards bigger goals. No matter what else you're saving for, the most important savings account is the one for your future – to either invest, buy a home or pay down debt. The main aim for the other savings accounts is to protect the future savings from being spent.

As a guide, saving 20% of your income over your working life will allow you to retire comfortably within around 30 years, provided those savings are invested in growth assets. If you're lucky enough to live without accommodation expenses (with family, for example), then it should be possible to save another 30% of your income, which is the amount most people spend on rent or a mortgage. Pete Adeney, who publishes under Mr Money Mustache, did a great analysis of the relationship between savings ratio and years to retirement, coming up with 64% as the magic proportion of income to save to be able to retire in just over ten years. Using his shockingly simple chart, 20% savings allows for retirement in 36.7 years.

Calculating how much you need to put into those accounts depends on how much you need and when. (The Golden Eggs web app has simple calculators to help with this.) For example, if you want to buy a $40,000 car in two years' time without taking out a loan, you'd better be saving $20,000 a year. Alternatively, aiming for a $30,000 car in three years cuts that down to $10,000 a year. As another example, if a normal holiday is $5000, but you plan to also take a $15,000 holiday in three years, then you might need to save $10,000 a year to cover both. I've set out this calculation in table 7.1.

Table 7.1: sample goal saving pattern

Goal	Cost	Frequency	Total to be saved per year
Normal holiday	$5000	1 year	$5000
Big trip	$15,000	3 years	$5000
Total			**$10,000**

You might be wondering about the extra benefits of interest on savings, but the savings interest will only give a small boost over a relatively short timeframe and will probably be offset by inflation. For example, 4% interest compounded over three years would increase total of the 'Big trip' savings by around $910, which is equivalent to a 2% annual increase in the money available for the trip.

Access and visibility

We all intuitively realise that the more money we can see and access, the higher the chance that we will spend it, whereas the more money we hide from ourselves – the less money we can see, the less money we can access – the less money we can spend impulsively.

We can limit our access to money by setting up a specific weekly spending account and having card access to this account only. If the only card you carry with you (either in your wallet or on your phone or watch) is linked to your weekly spending account, and that account receives a fixed amount of money, you can't go wrong.

The next challenge is visibility, because in the modern world we can instantly access money from almost anywhere with a few taps of a smartphone, especially if we can see all our other accounts with the same bank. The best way to counter this problem is to use double banking so that we only see the accounts in one bank (Bank B) – *not* the bank where we get paid, keep our savings and pay our bills (Bank A). Using the 'out of sight, out of mind' principle, most of us need to remove the bank app for Bank A. If the only app on our phone is for Bank B, with access to weekly spending money and fun money, then we are more likely to stick to our spending plan. Moving money from the fun account to the weekly account is fine, as both are for discretionary spending.

This means that to move money when we're out and about, we now must download the app, log in again and then try to move the money – engaging our System 2 thinking, which will hopefully make us realise that this is a bad idea.

Extra pay

Pay rises, bonuses and variable income are a common occurrence in many households. People often use variable income as a reason to not do any form of budgeting. In my experience, however, it's far better to estimate your average income (but be conservative) and then spend a consistent amount week to week and month to month. If you carry appropriate buffers in your bank account, there should be enough to make things work by the end of the year.

When you do get a windfall (especially a pay rise), as you have fixed the amount of money you spend you then have the option to spend more in a way that's more efficient. For example, having fixed their weekly and monthly spending, most people using the Fast and Slow System who then receive a pay rise equivalent to an extra $10,000 a year choose to focus first on their savings, second on having better holidays, then on having more fun and only consider having a little bit extra spending money every week last. Commonly, that looks like putting $5000 towards their mortgage or savings, spending an extra $2000 on making their next holiday better, adding $2400 a year ($200 a month) to the fun budget and then increasing the weekly budget by $600 a year (around $12 a week). In contrast, using most other systems (where regular savings are fixed) an extra $10,000 a year translates to around $200 a week, which most people simply spend on smaller stuff without realising.

Around nine months after my clients James and Bianca started implementing the Fast and Slow System, they called me to ask why they had over $5000 in their bills account rather than just their regular $1000 buffer. I suggested they check for upcoming bills, and they said that all the big bills had been paid. After further questioning, it turned out that James had received a decent pay rise four months earlier, but they hadn't adjusted their spending. This meant the funds just built up in their bills account while they decided what to do. This is a much better problem to have than finding savings haven't increased in several years of getting pay rises, which is what happened to my wife and I in our 20s, as well as to many others. James and Bianca decided to split the extra pay in a similar way to most people, putting more towards savings and holidays than towards their weekly and monthly spending plans.

In the next chapter I show you how you can personalise the Fast and Slow System so that it works for you.

Summary

- The Fast and Slow System is designed to help us hide our income and wealth from ourselves, like our ancestors did, and not walk around with instant access to all pay and savings.
- Double banking, which means using a different bank for discretionary spending than for bills and savings, makes it easier to control our spending.
- Giving ourselves fixed weekly spending money for our routines makes it easier to stick to a plan, with a monthly fun allowance arriving on the first of each month to allow us to live a little.

- Saving for multiple goals simultaneously is perfectly possible and will help with cutting back on thc small things. It's also easier to save for things two to five years out than leaving it to the last minute.
- When pay is separated from spending, extra pay will only be spent when you decide to move the money. Use System 2 thinking to choose wisely!

Chapter 8

Personalised design

When it comes to personal finances, there is no one-size-fits-all solution. However, we can apply certain rules universally. As I discussed in the previous chapter, these rules include:

1. separating pay and bills into an account that cannot be accessed with a card or for daily transactions
2. maintaining a level of financial autonomy when in a relationship, so each partner has their own money to spend
3. adapting automations of amounts transferred to each person's accessible accounts to align with personal psychology, allocating weekly funds for routine expenses and monthly funds for fun and non-weekly discretionary expenses.
4. saving for multiple goals simultaneously in different accounts.

Even while following these rules, various permutations of the system – such as having individual or joint fun accounts and determining who pays the bills in a relationship – can be implemented to suit the user's individual situation. To better understand this and then put the most suitable version of the system to use, it's essential that you first examine your money personality (and your partner's, if you have one).

Money personalities

Most individuals fall into three broad categories of money personality, based on their upbringing and past experiences. There are those who hate to spend, those who love to spend and those who don't mind spending occasionally. We can further categorise these individuals into five designations: tight-arses, savers, balanced, spenders and shopaholics.

Tight-arses are Scrooges who genuinely hate spending money. They often have a past trauma related to money and feel physically uncomfortable when spending. For these individuals, most purchasing decisions are rational and carefully considered. These people are sometimes described as having 'short arms and deep pockets'. Often, they'll leave the pub before it's their round.

As I explained at the start of this book, I'm a tight-arse, through and through. I grew up in a family of nine kids, where money was in short supply, and our mum always said, 'Waste not, want not'. We were raised to not to want for things and to look down on other children getting fancy gifts or buying new stuff all the time. That way we wouldn't be disappointed when we didn't get similar things, and we'd be pleasantly surprised if we did. Where tight-arses struggle in the world is not wanting to waste money on experiences that they could thoroughly enjoy and in letting go of the purse-strings to spend on gifts for others or make charitable donations. They can also struggle in relationships with spenders and shopaholics, getting quite anxious over every transaction they can see that doesn't fit with their own values.

Savers are a milder version of tight-arses. While they enjoy the process of saving, they are less likely to feel anxious about spending money on necessary items. That said, like tight-arses, they can still miss out on a lot of life's fun by focusing too much on saving.

At the other end of the spectrum are **shopaholics**, who buy items compulsively and often have personal loans and credit card debts. These individuals are driven by impulses, making purchases without considering the consequences. Though there is a lot of evidence that buying stuff doesn't necessarily make us happier, shopaholics' behaviour might stem from unhappiness, trauma in their lives or a difficult upbringing.

My wife falls into this category. Like me, Kelly was raised in a household with very little money, but in her household it was normal to gamble. That meant even less money, but every now and then there was a win! The win meant suddenly the food was better, the washing machine got replaced and there were new clothes and gifts. Many people with similar formative experiences felt that if they had money then it was best to spend it fast, because they never knew when more might be coming. In Kelly's upbringing, there was also an ingrained need for her to not appear poor and to demonstrate this to other people by wearing nice clothes and having nice things. System 1 thinking is very much the usual setting for shopaholics. A little like gamblers, they're looking for the dopamine hit of buying something and not really thinking about the consequences. Lots of them have stories about how they've even tried to fool themselves and their partners into thinking that they hadn't really done anything bad.

Spenders are to shopaholics what savers are to tight-arses. Spenders enjoy spending money and, like shopaholics, they get that thrill of spending and their impulse control isn't great. However, they are more likely than shopaholics to have boundaries and not cross them. They generally have less credit card debt and lower personal loans.

Balanced is the middle ground. These people spend a bit and save a bit, but they're not strongly engaged in one behaviour or the other. This makes them susceptible to System 1 overspending while also being capable of building up savings over time.

Each of the five personalities benefit in different ways from the Fast and Slow System. Tight arses don't really need any help to control their spending, but having a budget for holidays and fun makes them feel less anxious about enjoying life. It also improves relationships, as their partners have an agreed amount to spend, and they can still reach their shared goals. This relieves stress and reduces arguments.

Shopaholics and spenders need some structure in their lives. Rather than trying to berate or educate shopaholics and spenders into spending less, their physical card will tell them when they've overdone things. It's far better for them to try to make a purchase and have their card decline, so they know they're about to go over budget, than to overspend (with or without realising), because then it'll be too late.

Having implemented the Fast and Slow System, my wife has her own spending account and knows she has money to spend. It's also entirely her decision what she spends that money on. More importantly, there will be more money next week. This means even if she spends all the money in the first part of the week, she only needs to wait a few more days for more. From there, she can create a list of things she's interested in for the next week or month. It's a good way for her to feel she can get the things she wants; she just has to prioritise and then make a choice. After all, if something is always getting pushed down the priority list, it's probably a good thing it wasn't bought in the first place.

Two tight-arses together will find that they'll get more out of life if they agree to spend some money on experiences, gifts and connecting with others than if they lean into their natural tendencies to save every cent. Agreeing on a budget for each will allow them to let go a little bit every now and then. This is similar with a couple of savers, and also the combination of saver and tight-arse, because it helps them to know it's OK to save to spend later or enjoy themselves along the way and build great memories. We don't want to be on our deathbeds regretting not enjoying ourselves a little bit while we were younger.

Things get interesting when we put the two most different money personalities together: tight-arses (such as me) and shopaholics (such as Kelly). It's important that the shopaholic has some boundaries, but also the tight-arse needs to know that there's no point getting upset about how much things cost because they were within the agreed spending plan. When paired with a tight-arse or saver, a shopaholic or spender needs a good-sized monthly fun budget. They should also probably take control of the grocery budget to give themselves an incentive to cut back and have more for what they'd prefer to be spending on. Most tight-arses and savers don't need a fun budget if their partner has one, so long as they're comfortable asking their partner to buy them clothes or for money to buy gifts.

The slightly trickier combinations are balanced with shopaholic and spender with shopaholic. If they don't personalise their structure so that it works for them as a couple, it's likely that the shopaholic will consistently overspend and the other will argue with them about it while wanting to do some of the spending themselves. Experience has taught me that the balanced, spender and shopaholic categories of money personality need their own fun budgets. It sounds counterintuitive to give funds to the person who wants to spend, but in most relationships it's far better to give each other some freedom within the bounds of an overall household spending plan than cut off supply altogether. Personally, I don't have a fun budget and I haven't bought anything for years, because that would deprive my wife of the fun of going out and buying stuff – even stuff *for* me. I would just feel anxious about it, so why should I go to the shops when Kelly enjoys the process much more?

System management

If you're not in a relationship, the responsibility obviously falls to you and you alone. However, in a couple, it's crucial that each person has their own areas of responsibility, with different accounts delegated accordingly.

Generally, the bills budget should be managed by the more frugal person in the relationship. If there's a tight-arse, then they should be the one to manage bills. In cases where one person is a shopaholic and the other is a spender, it might be best for the spender to manage the bills, since they're less likely to use bill money for other purposes. The same principle applies to savings accounts. The more frugal person in the relationship typically ensures that savings stay on track. However, if you're saving for a holiday, once you go on holiday that budget should be transferred to the person who most loves to spend, with the caveat that food and accommodation must be covered first. Otherwise, the more frugal person should keep back some funds to make sure there's enough to last the whole trip, and the less frugal one will make sure they have a damn good time with the rest!

The spending budget, on the other hand, is best placed in the hands of the person who most wants to spend. This approach allows them to learn and grow within a system that accommodates their natural tendencies while also providing a clear cut-off.

Some people feel the concept of setting a budget and an 'allowance' is controlling and manipulative. It's important to note that this system aims to replicate the way many families manage money, where one person takes on financial management and the other receives an agreed-upon amount to spend. However, there can be a dark side to this approach.

If it becomes controlling or without mutual agreement and shared goals, then it goes too far. In such cases, one person may assume control of all finances, leaving the other in the dark and without a say in financial matters. I don't advocate any form of financial abuse, which this would be a clear case of. Please make sure to discuss your goals and overall spending plan together, and make sure each member of the partnership has their say. Practically, households tend to work better when the roles I've just discussed are separated, so make sure to both agree on who will manage and pay the bills, and who will pay for groceries and pocket the leftovers. We'll revisit this in chapter 11, along with an example of what to do if you're in a couple and not ready to fully merge finances.

So, how does all this look in practice? Here are some examples of how it works.

Single: Balanced, saving for house deposit, holiday and car

James is an IT graduate who has moved out of home and is renting, but he wants to save up to buy his first home, as well as upgrade his car and take nice holidays. He's OK with saving, but he has a history of spending most of his savings. James's structure still has 20% of his income going towards his future but with enough also going into accounts for holidays and a new car, in line with the timing of his goals. His weekly spending is enough to get by, with a decent fun budget to allow more creativity with activities that can't be achieved with the weekly budget alone (see figure 8.1). He will probably get best results using a cash management account for his bills, which we cover in more detail in chapter 11.

Figure 8.1: James's sample structure

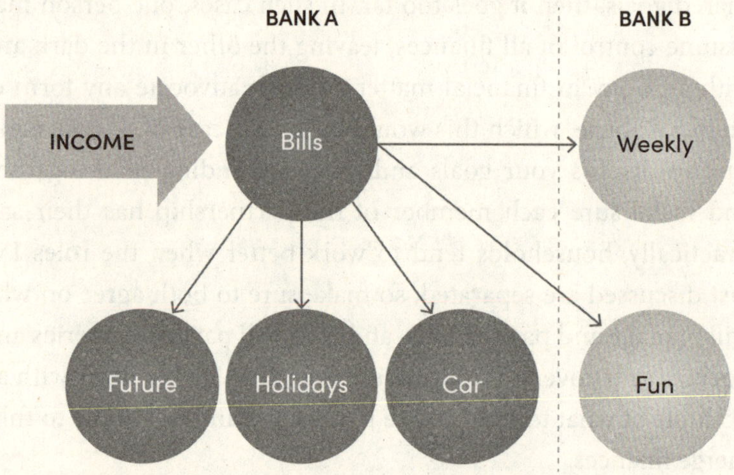

Couple: Saver and spender, saving to upgrade to a family home and for holiday and car

Sam is a spender, so they have the grocery money in their weekly allowance. They also control the fun money. Alex has a smaller weekly allowance, with enough to cover an occasional lunch or coffee. Sam pays when they both go out and covers all the gift spending. Sam now knows that shopping at Aldi and looking for bargains elsewhere leaves more money for entertainment. Alex manages bills and savings and is less likely to get stressed by holiday spending and Sam's fun spending if they're within the spending plan. They will repurpose their joint account as the new bills account (where they'll be paid), as they already have most bills coming from it (see figure 8.2).

Figure 8.2: Sam and Alex's sample structure

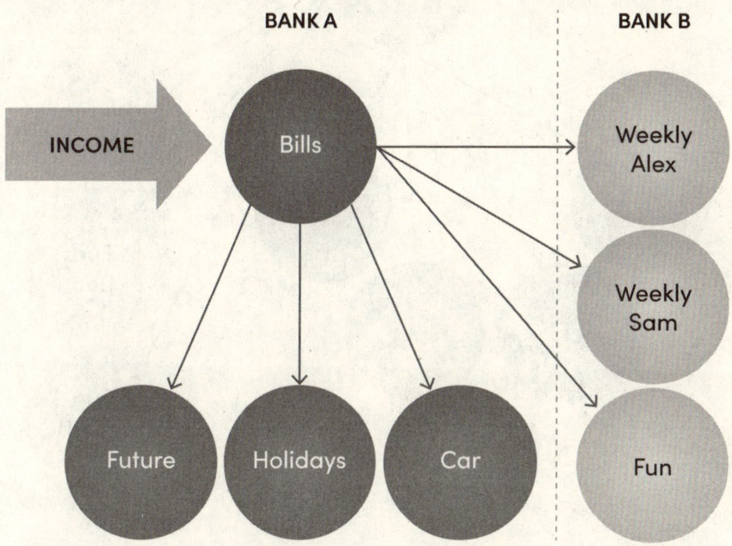

Couple: Balanced and spender, saving for first home, wedding, holiday and car

Ben is balanced but still needs a fun budget, whereas Matt likes to spend, so he has a slightly bigger fun budget as well as responsibility for groceries. They plan to get married next year, and they're also saving for a new car, so they have extra savings accounts (see figure 8.3, overleaf). Ben manages bills and savings. They needed a little help from a money coach to get set up and work out the spending plan properly, and they'll use a new cash management account for their bills (see chapter 11).

Figure 8.3: Ben and Matt's sample structure

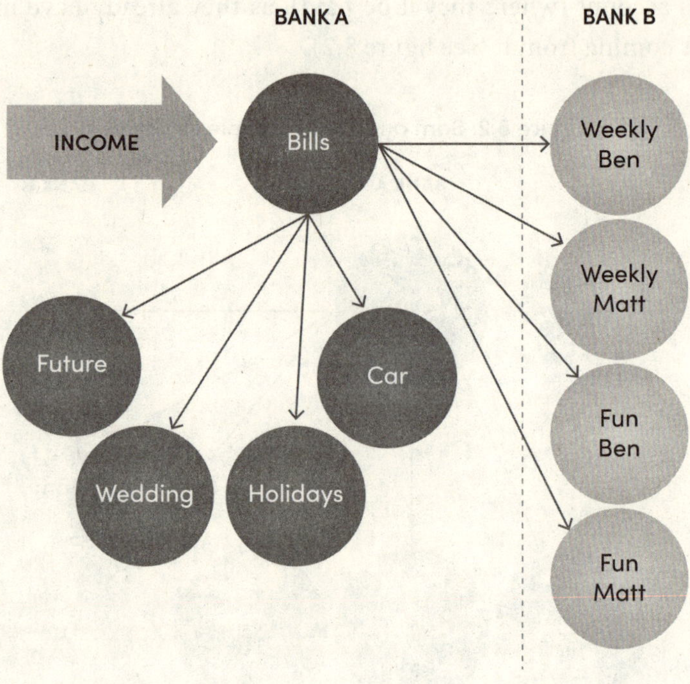

Businesses, side businesses and variable incomes

Many people run their own businesses or side hustles and don't have a stable, regular income. This can make budgeting seem difficult or even impossible. However, as a business owner, I find that having a spending plan is even more crucial when income is variable.

The goal of the Fast and Slow System is to set a fixed level for discretionary or variable spending and then stick to it. The first step when you have a side or main business is to ensure that you're managing it in accounts that are kept separate from any of the other accounts we've discussed so far. This helps to prevent accidental overspending by restricting access to funds. Ideally, the business accounts should be held at a different bank to your personal spending accounts. This is particularly important if your side hustle involves an investment property. I recommend that rental income lands in its own account and all associated bills, such as mortgage and council rates, are paid from that separate account. This simplifies things and allows you to see if the account balance is growing or shrinking, indicating whether you're making or losing money.

The same approach applies to businesses. In the early stages, the business account will have income and expenses, and profits may be minimal. The best way to measure profit is by monitoring cash flow and checking if there's more money coming in than going out. As the business matures and reaches a level of predictable income, you can begin transferring a set amount from the business account to your personal account. However, you need more than just one business account. You should have at least one additional account for taxes. When transferring money from your business to your personal account, remember that a portion of it will need to be set aside for goods and services tax (GST) and income tax. If you don't allocate funds for taxes, you may face a large tax bill at the end of the year. Managing cash-based businesses can be challenging, but the solution is straightforward: simply use an envelope system, like my parents and possibly your grandparents used, to allocate money for different purposes. This ensures that you only spend what's allowed and set aside enough for taxes.

The key question is about how much money you should allocate to the budget from a business. It's best to budget conservatively, planning for the lower end of your expected income range. For example, if you think your business will generate between $50,000 and $100,000 in a year, budget for $50,000. This way, if you exceed your expectations, it's a pleasant surprise rather than a shortfall. Establish a regular payment into your bills account and allocate funds for the weekly account first. As your income grows, you can adjust your budget for fun and holidays accordingly, but always ensure a portion is set aside for potential future downturns. In chapter 11 we'll review an example of handling income above the minimum, bonuses and pay rises.

In the next chapter we'll look at practical examples of how the Fast and Slow System plays out.

Summary

- It's important to adjust your banking structure to suit your personality – or, if in a couple, each individual's personality – and then manage the system in a way that's most likely to work.
- We're all a bit different with money, and knowing where you and your partner sit on a scale from tight-arse to shopaholic makes it easier for the two of you to allocate and control spending.
- The more likely you are to spend, the more autonomy you should be given through weekly and fun budgets. The person in a couple who is least likely to spend should manage bills and savings.
- If income is variable, or you're managing a business, sticking to the spending plan is even more critical, with business income and expenses kept separate from personal.

Chapter 9

Making it all add up

Sometimes, when we add up all the figures in our budget, we find that things don't quite add up as they should. Perhaps our total expenses exceed our total income, or the leftover amount is too small a proportion of our income for adequate savings. As a reminder, the goal is to save around 20% of our income – or, without accommodation expenses, around 50% of our income. Alternatively, we can aim for half our income minus whatever we're spending on rent or mortgage repayments.

There could be various reasons for this discrepancy, but one significant factor is that our regular weekly and monthly expenses might be higher than necessary, leaving us with insufficient funds for holidays or saving up for other goals, such as a car. We might attribute this to the cost of living, but as Australia's minimum wage legislation is designed to ensure that people earn more than enough to cover basic living expenses, the issue usually lies elsewhere.

In this chapter, we'll discuss prioritising goals and re-evaluating what's important in life. This may involve making both big-picture and small-picture cutbacks. We also need to examine the impact of certain liabilities, such as repaying personal loans or car loans, on our overall financial situation. Once we've gone through all the elements to determine where we can make cutbacks, we might still find that our current savings rate isn't what it needs to be. In this case, we can consider Richard H Thaler and Cass R Sunstein's 'Save More Tomorrow' concept – a well-researched and documented approach that involves gradually increasing the proportion of our pay that goes into savings over time, rather than increasing our spending with our pay.

The Fast and Slow System fixes variable spending, and inertia plus laziness means that as we get pay rises, we rarely increase the amounts we give ourselves. This means we literally save more as our pay goes up over time. It will initially default to building up in the bills account, but allocating the extra to savings until the 20% saving target is hit is ideal.

What you're really spending: Mitch and Grace

On a warm autumn evening in Sydney, Mitch and Grace arrived at their first appointment with me, their mortgage broker. They felt slightly nervous about how much money they might be able to borrow and whether their savings would be enough to buy a property. They were also anxious about their plans to start a family in the not-too-distant future and the impact that taking on a huge amount of debt would have on their lives.

At 29 and 22 respectively, Mitch and Grace were relatively young to be married, and it was surprising to learn that they wanted to have kids soon. With $20,000 in savings and needing help from their parents to buy their first property, they were finally having the conversation they'd been dreading. Could they afford to buy something?

I asked how much they spent each month. Mitch and Grace said they spent around $3000, plus $1000 in rent ($4000 in total).

I then asked how much they earned each month. They said that together they made $10,000 a month. When asked about their monthly savings, they said they tried to save around $2000 but sometimes dipped into it. I pointed out that if they were earning $10,000 and saving $2000, they were spending $8000 a month, not $4000.

Mitch and Grace went on to a full money coaching program and implemented the Fast and Slow System immediately. As a result, just three years later, they're now paying down their first property and have already bought an investment, all while starting a family. They now fully control their expenses and are building up their savings to buy a family car and go on a holiday.

My conversation with Mitch and Grace is typical of many others I've had with people who were surprised to learn what they *really* spend, as opposed to what they *thought* they spent. I know this pattern well from when my wife and I were in our 20s. As I explained in chapter 2, every year we'd create a budget and plan our savings, only to fall short. It wasn't until we were in our 30s that we fixed the issue. I sympathise with anyone in a similar situation and, since becoming a broker in 2009, I have done my very best to help people change in the same way that Kelly and I did. The more I read and study, the better I understand the problems many people face in their 20s and 30s, and sometimes even through their entire lives. I've made it my life's mission to help people get on track sooner rather than later.

Back to goals: Carol and James

No, this isn't a football reference; we're talking about revisiting our goals and looking at the amount of money those goals might take. When we cost our goals, one of the biggest factors is the amount of money we plan to spend on the goal and when we plan to achieve it.

For example, if you think you'd like to take a $20,000 holiday in two years, that's going to cost you $10,000 a year for the next two years. But if that's going to hurt the budget too much and you can only put $5000 a year towards a holiday, then you either need to wait four years before taking a $20,000 holiday or consider taking a $10,000 holiday in two years. The same goes for other big-ticket items, such as cars. What you absolutely don't want to do is delete a goal or borrow money to hit a spending goal. You must look at all the other elements of the budget first to see if you can cut back on something else to make room for that goal.

When I first met Carol and James, they were in a great financial position due to the property they acquired when they were younger. They had benefited from capital growth, but when we looked at how long it would take them to pay off their mortgage, we found that if they carried on spending at their current rate they would get there in around 20 years. However, by spending according to the principles I've outlined in this book, they could clear the mortgage in around 12 years.

When they first planned out their weekly spending, they assumed that they would spend $300 on groceries and then another $200 on other regular weekly expenses: $500 a week. I knew that the average grocery spend for a family in their situation was between $150 and $240 a week, so planning to spend $300 seemed excessive. I also knew that weekly money is usually just frittered away on small things that don't add value to people's lives. Instead, I suggested a budget of $400 a week, *including* regular expenses. That hundred-dollar-a-week saving is worth $5200 per year, which is a significant amount of money to put towards another more important goal, such as paying down a mortgage.

Another important goal many people have is debt reduction. As discussed in chapter 5, your net position is assets minus liabilities, so you can either build up a savings account as an asset or pay down debt. For that reason, when we're making things balance, we don't include the repayment of the debt in our regular bills. We just include the interest cost, because the interest cost is the actual cost of the money. Anything on top of the interest is like savings, putting us further ahead.

When it comes to bills, the biggest cutback we can make is on something like rent or the amount of interest we're paying on a mortgage. Living in a more expensive place means a higher cost of rent or repayments on a much bigger mortgage. Of course, we can ask for an interest rate reduction on any mortgage we take, but the decision to borrow $800,000 for a $1 million property or $1.8 million for a $2 million property will have a far greater impact on overall costs than the interest rate. Remember, this is a choice we must make, and we should balance that against other choices. If living in a fancy house now is going to stop us from buying our own fancy house in the future, then it's often easier to make the transition to a cheaper place now, knowing that we'll get to a better place in the future.

Other cutbacks can be made in areas such as regular bills for electricity, phones, gas and insurance. Simply comparing, switching providers or negotiating a discount with your existing provider can save money. The same goes for mortgage interest rates. Usually, you can negotiate a better deal on your existing mortgage every year. If you don't, chances are you're paying more than someone else would. Any of these cutbacks allows more money to go towards savings or other future goals.

Too much rent: Tammy

Tammy, a strong, independent woman, loves to go out and party. My wife and I are quite social too, and we met Tammy through a mutual friend at a live band karaoke bar one night. We had the usual bar chat about our jobs, and she expressed interest in learning how to save more money to buy her own place. We exchanged contact information and agreed to meet up when we were all sober.

Tammy earned a decent income, and she enjoyed going out, driving a nice car and spending her money. However, she knew she wasn't saving as much as she should be and wasn't able to buy a place. When she examined her budget in detail, she discovered that the two most significant expenses that were challenging to reduce were rent and car payments. We'll look at car payments soon; for now, though, let's focus on the rent. As I've mentioned before, people typically spend about 30% of their income on rent or their mortgage, but Tammy spent over 40% on rent alone. If she continued to spend that much on rent, it would be extremely difficult for her to save up enough money to buy her own place and escape the rent cycle.

Tammy's options were to stay where she was and take a long time to save up for a deposit, move to a more affordable place by herself, or get a flatmate to share the cost of her current residence. After careful consideration, Tammy decided to rent a cheaper place by herself, so she wouldn't have to rely on someone else's money and deal with the potential conflicts and inconveniences that come from living with others. This was the first significant compromise she made in her lifestyle, but she understood it was necessary if she wanted to make progress and own her place in the future. By reducing her rent to around 28% of her income instead of over 40%, Tammy was able to achieve her goal of saving 20% of her income, giving her a clear timeline for saving enough to buy her own place.

In Sydney and other major cities, where rent is a significantly higher portion of income relative to average incomes in other cities, it's more common for singles to face this issue than it is for couples. Rents aren't that high when there are at least two people in the household. During the peak COVID-19 years, many people experienced heightened need for personal space and less interaction with others. Many flatmates moved out to get their own place, and while many couples started looking for larger homes, numerous relationships broke down. All of this contributed to a shortage in housing, not just in capital cities such as Sydney but also in regional centres, driving up rents. Rents have also increased since 2022 with rising migration levels and escalating interest rates, and people are realising the economic benefits of sharing their home to reduce the average cost per person rather than having their own space just in case of another lockdown. It makes no practical sense for two people to have a two-bedroom unit each when they could share and have a room each for half the price. This is an example of a seemingly illogical and irrational decision being made because it feels like we need more space and independence. It's a classic case of our emotional System 1 thinking winning out.

The cost of kids

When I was a 24-year-old father of two, working as a marketing assistant, I remember a senior marketing manager in her early 30s, expecting her first child, asking me how much extra she should budget for. She reasoned that they don't eat much, so she estimated that a few dollars a week should cover it. I had to laugh, and my answer now hasn't changed much from my answer then. Kids will cost everything you choose to spend on them – the more you have, the more you're likely to spend.

Normally it starts out with finding a bigger home, then kitting out that home with a cot, change table, clothes, toys, nappies and all the other things you imagine you'll need. Pretty quickly you realise that the clothes are outgrown within weeks, most toys are ignored, disposable nappies seem in endless demand and there's other weird stuff too, like breast pumps, sterilisers, baby monitors, nappy rash cream and teething aids – a world of stuff you'd never heard of. Then, if you're coupled and both return to work, early childhood education and care (ECEC) costs can easily become the biggest source of expenditure. Often, parents end up working three or four days a week for years, meaning it can take a long time to get back to full income again.

Marketers tug on our heartstrings so we buy their products to show we care for our little ones. Yet talk to any parent who bought everything brand new and they'll tell you it's a waste of money. They're often trying to give away the stuff that's cluttering up their homes! Kelly and I were lucky to have kids when we were young and had less money, so we had to do things on the cheap, but even then we spent way too much and gave away lots of stuff. Our eldest children were my parents' first grandkids, and we have photos of the next four of their cousins all wearing the same outfits that were handed down from us to my sisters' kids and then the next sister.

If you become a parent, please accept all kind donations and gifts from family and friends, and preserve your own money for what's important. Also, try to create routines for grandparents to spend time with kids, which will help cut ECEC costs. Kelly and I loved having our grandson on Mondays, Tuesdays and

Fridays, but more than two days in a row became too exhausting. Spacing out the days helped, as did the other grandparents taking him on Thursdays, leaving his parents with only one day a week to manage. ECEC costs can be huge and often pause our savings in the years when we need to be saving the most. Once we see the costs as temporary, it becomes easier to accept it's just until they start school.

School fees are a huge additional expense that I've never quite wrapped my head around. In Australia, we have a three-tiered school system, with public schools (free, except for voluntary contributions, uniforms, textbooks and after-school stuff), Catholic schools (around Sydney, this could be anywhere from $2000 to $15,000 a year) and private schools (from $10,000 to $45,000 a year, again around Sydney).

There are plenty of studies exploring the differences (and lack thereof) between private- and public-school outcomes, but many of us will end up making an emotional decision to give our kids opportunities that we feel are either the same or better than we had, which can mean sending them to non-government schools. These fees are reasonably predictable, regardless of the chosen system or systems, so we can estimate the total cost over a child's school life to calculate the impact on our finances. Working this out before they start in a system is best, so we have an idea of what we're in for.

Depending on what you choose to do, it may simply be a case of coming to terms with knowing that your savings will be hit for that amount of time. For example, if you decide to choose a local Catholic school with annual fees of $7000, then 13 years of schooling will likely cost $91,000 for each child. Compare this to a $40,000-a-year private school, which will cost $520,000 over all 13 years or $240,000 over just the six years of high school.

The great car-loan con

Imagine being tasked with selling $50,000 cars in a country where people think a $30,000 car is a stretch. If someone saves $110 a week for five years, they have around $31,600 (assuming 4% yearly compounding interest – enough to buy a $30,000 car plus on-road costs and insurance. But what if you could persuade people to put $190 a week toward a $50,000 car and get it today? Rationally, using System 2 thinking, that's a terrible decision, as it increases our outgoings by 73% (from $110 to $190), to buy a depreciating asset we don't even own. We're just borrowing the money to buy that car. However, our emotional System 1 thinking tells us that we really want that $50,000 car. The seats are comfier, the brand is nicer and it's the car we've always wanted. It's only $80 a week extra (as opposed to savings), so surely we can treat ourselves, right?

That's how the luxury car market works in Australia. We're upsold from a car we could afford to buy outright in a few years, so we're locked into a finance repayment. Typically, to buy that $50,000 car, dealerships will offer finance with a 40% balloon payment, which means that at the end of the four-year term we must pay the $20,000 balloon. Alternatively, we could trade the car for around $20,000 and upgrade again. Essentially, for that $190 a week over four years, we've just paid the interest and depreciation on the car and effectively rented it.

A rational thought process would suggest that we should save up $20,000 in four years to pay off the car, but most of us don't work that way. Instead, we get to the end of the four years and the dealer contacts us again, offering to trade in the $20,000 car for a brand new $50,000 car if we sign up for $190 a week for the next four years. This cycle continues, locking in $190 a week in revenue for the dealership for as long as we're working and earning money.

An alternative course of action is to be patient. If we take that $190 a week and put it into a savings account, delaying the gratification of having a new car, we'll have over $30,000 after three years. With this money, we can buy a three-year-old car equivalent to the $50,000 car we could've bought initially. The difference is we now own that car outright.

Imagine two people: Hayden and Tyler. Hayden signs up for a four-year car loan with a 40% balloon payment, paying $190 a week to drive a $50,000 car today. In three years, Hayden is still driving that car and making a weekly payment of $190. Meanwhile, three years after starting to put away the same amount in savings each week, Tyler is able to buy a car identical to Hayden's outright, and for the next 12 months she's driving the same car as him – without any car payments. Most new cars come with five- to eight-year warranties, so there's nothing stopping Tyler from buying a three- or four-year-old car, driving it until it's seven or eight years old, then selling it privately and upgrading to another three- or four-year-old car. The difference between Hayden and Tyler is that Hayden is now a slave to the $190 a week repayment, while it costs Tyler less and less to upgrade her car. Assuming she buys at three years old, sells at eight years and buys a three-year-old car again, she'd only need to save $70 a week after the initial purchase to be able to upgrade again.

Better than saving up for a three-year-old luxury car is not buying into the 'luxury' car con at all. Warren Buffett, one of the world's richest people, advises buying a modest car. He doesn't buy an expensive car for himself because he knows it's a depreciating asset. Instead, it's better to put that $190 a week into appreciating assets, which eventually generate enough income through returns, dividends or rental income to buy whatever car you want later in life. In contrast, many people continue the new-car treadmill until they reach retirement. Then, realising they can no longer afford the car payment, they have to use super to make the balloon payment and then make their final car last for the next 20 or 30 years. By instead being financially disciplined and focusing on appreciating assets rather than depreciating ones, you can achieve long-term financial stability and success. This approach allows you to enjoy the things you want in life without becoming a slave to ongoing payments and financial stress.

In summary, the great car-loan con is a perfect example of how emotional System 1 thinking can result in us making irrational and financially detrimental decisions. By being aware of this and relying more on rational System 2 thinking, we can make better choices for our financial future, leading to a more secure and fulfilling life.

'Save More Tomorrow'

'Save More Tomorrow' is an ingenious concept, developed by economist Richard H Thaler and legal scholar Cass R Sunstein, that leverages our inherent laziness with money. The idea is to commit to maintaining our current level of expenditure while allocating a certain percentage of any future pay rises towards a savings account.

This approach has been successfully implemented in the US, where companies encourage employees to sign agreements stipulating that an increasing percentage of their pay rises will go towards their retirement funds. In Australia, a similar concept was introduced through our compulsory superannuation scheme. The scheme began with 4.5% of each employee's pay being directed towards a retirement fund and has increased over time to 11% in July 2023, with plans to eventually reach 12% by 2025.

You can apply the Save More Tomorrow concept outside of superannuation to save up for other goals, such as buying a home. If it's not possible to achieve a 20% savings goal, aim for at least 10% to begin with, and have a plan to increase this percentage with expected increases in income, reductions in expenses such as ECEC and HECS, or changes in work situations.

The long-term benefit of separating expenditure from income is that as income grows, more funds can be allocated towards savings rather than expenses. This idea is reminiscent of the teachings of George S Clason, who suggests saving at least 10% of our income. In his book *The Richest Man in Babylon* he argues that when we commit to saving and see our wealth grow, we are more likely to take on extra work or invest our income to further increase our savings.

By committing to long-term wealth-building we can gain the motivation to save more and work towards our financial goals, such as buying a home or an investment property. In a US study on the efficacy of the Save More Tomorrow concept, the average savings rate increased from 8% to 13%. By implementing this strategy ourselves, we can harness our inherent financial tendencies to work towards a more secure and fulfilling financial future.

Summary

- On a first attempt at a budget or spending plan it can be difficult to hit the 20% target, but if we persevere, make adjustments on the way and avoid getting sucked into things that take us off track, the results are worth it.
- Trying to hit too many big spending goals at the expense of future savings can be fixed by delaying spending or reducing the total cost of these goals.

- Housing is a big cost, so adjusting your plan (for example, by getting a housemate or moving to a cheaper area) to take this cost to no more than 30% of income could be worthwhile.
- Kids will cost as much as we choose to spend on them, but ECEC and loss of income can be our biggest challenges and make our goals for future savings impossible for a few years. However, the shortfall has a predictable end date.
- Cars are typically our biggest discretionary spending items and getting sucked into buying new, luxury cars can ruin a perfectly good plan. It's better to save up and buy outright than take on a loan.
- When all else fails, the Save More Tomorrow concept lets you automatically increase savings in the future as circumstances change or temporary expenses disappear.

Chapter 10
Credit card addiction

In chapter 1, we saw that the modern banking system has almost entirely removed the friction in spending, meaning there is little to interrupt the idea of buying something turning into the action of buying it. Credit cards are a leading cause of spending fast, with all countries seeing a drop in savings rates from 1975 to 2005, coinciding with the rise in credit card use over the same period. The implication is that the more you use a credit card, the less you'll save. In the context of the Fast and Slow System, credit cards are a system leak that makes it impossible to control spending. Debit cards linked to a fixed spending amount will decline when the money runs out. Credit cards keep saying 'approved' up to their limit, and even people who claim to be good at sticking to a budget sometimes carry a balance from one month to the next.

Most of us don't think we're addicted. To find out, just try giving up your credit card for the next three months. If you're not addicted, you'll be fine. However, if you start making excuses to avoid even starting the three-month trial, you're behaving like an addict. The question is, is this addiction harmful? I used to think I was careful with my credit card, always paying it off in full each month. However, looking back, I see that I was addicted. More importantly, it was hurting our finances.

Credit cards were invented to avoid embarrassment when we couldn't afford our bills, but now we use them for everything. Our rational brain should ask why we're borrowing money for everyday expenses, but our intuitive thinking justifies it, assuming we'll pay it off at the end of the month and it's all the same money.

In this chapter, we'll investigate the psychology behind credit card use and explore studies that show how foolish we can be. We'll also debunk some myths about points and interest savings. It's important that we cover this now, because credit card use is the biggest problem I see anyone encounter when trying to commit to a savings plan. In my experience, people will be unable to achieve their goals if they're using a credit card regularly – and in this chapter you'll see why.

The psychology of credit card use

There have been many studies on credit card usage over the past few decades that we can learn from. One important aspect of credit cards is that they decouple the pain of paying from the pleasure of receiving. When we have cash – or a limited amount of funds in a spending account – we know how much we have, and every time we buy something we feel the money disappearing. This is what psychologists call 'the pain of paying'. Other forms of credit, such as personal loans and buy now pay later schemes, are generally linked to a specific item. This means that even if these credit options encourage us to buy things we don't have the money for, at least when we feel the pain of the repayments we know what it was for. With dozens of purchases on credit card, it's much harder to isolate what the bill is for.

When using a credit card, two separate concepts come into play. First is the way we perceive an individual purchase relative to our available funds. Essentially, a $70 expense is likely to feel like a significant portion of a $250 weekly allowance but only a small fraction of an expected $4000 credit card bill. This changes our perception of the impact of our spending, making it easier to spend more because everything is small compared to our limit or monthly bill.

The second concept is the notional limit we set for ourselves on our credit card. While the credit card might have a $10,000 limit, if our salary is only $7000 and we have $2000 of rent to pay, we might feel uncomfortable going over a self-imposed limit of, say, $4000 to $4500. As a result, we keep spending up to that notional amount and only then try to stop spending. Unfortunately, if the credit card bill for the month then comes in at $5000, we get worried about how we're going to pay the bill and cover the rent.

We know that we don't look at our credit card transactions with the System 2, analytical part of our brain. Instead, we use System 1, intuitive thinking to try to find a shortcut. There might be a hundred or so transactions, but naturally we look for big expenses. Maybe we'll find the quarterly electricity bill that came due at the end of the month or a weekend away when we spent money on the hotel. If that satisfies our System 1 thinking, we stop looking and just assume it won't happen again. If we itemise everything, however, we might find it wasn't the $700 electricity bill, since that was always due, but maybe it was the $500 we spent on takeaway on top of $400 on lunches and snacks. Back when Kelly and I used a credit card, it would be school uniforms one month, the electricity bill another month, Christmas, holidays, someone's birthday… around 10 months out of 12 the bill would be higher than we thought it should have been.

Numerous studies have shown that people who use a credit card spend more than people who don't or who use cash. One famous study found that participants were willing to spend 114% more on the same item when they used a credit card versus using cash, while a recent study of brain activity showed that using a credit card activates the reward networks in the brain regardless of price. An Australian Government report found that people underestimate the probability that they will pay interest on their credit cards. Other studies have reached similar conclusions, showing that average spend is 35% higher with credit cards than with cash and 8% higher when using a credit card close to its limit.

In the example I gave a little earlier, we were trying to set ourselves a target of $4000 to $4500, yet the average Australian couple only spends $2550 on non-housing essentials per month. This means that this target of $4000 to $4500 is actually a planned $1450 to $2050 discretionary spend per month. In my personal and professional experience, cutting up the credit cards can reduce discretionary spending by around half, leading to 25% to 30% lower spending overall.

If you still believe that you're not like everyone else and that you are a responsible credit card user, try going without it for three months as I suggested earlier. The difference it'll make in your points or savings balance is quite small in the context of a whole year, but you might learn something by just taking the credit card out of your wallet, unlinking it from your devices and leaving it at home. See what happens when you try to spend your own money instead of borrowing money. Only if you pass a trial of three months can you honestly say you're not like everyone else.

Cutting up the cards: Rob and Claire

When I first met Rob and Claire, they were in a great financial position overall thanks to some astute property investments before the booms and Rob's very high income. Rob's income meant that they didn't see the sense in trying to budget. They were happy to put everything on their credit card every month and loved the flight upgrades from their points.

In our coaching sessions, I showed them that at their current rate of spending at 45, they would be debt free by age 70, whereas changing to the Fast and Slow System could see them hit the same target by age 60. If you're under 30, you might think there's not much difference between 60 and 70, but for those hoping to retire comfortably before they get too old, 60 is a much more appealing option.

The credit cards were initially hidden away and removed from phones while we experimented with weekly and monthly spending plans. The drop in weekly spending was the harshest and caused the most adjustment, but within a month it was their new normal. A year later, they couldn't believe how fast their mortgage had dropped, and even when Rob got another pay rise they opted not to increase their weekly allowances as they had realised how much pointless small stuff they'd gotten into the habit of saying 'no' to since making the change. They'd decided it was much better to increase the holiday budget and add a Christmas account than have more to waste week to week.

Why points don't help

The most common justification I hear for keeping credit cards is the allure of reward points, particularly those that can be cashed in for flights. After all, who doesn't love a free flight? There's an underlying assumption that credit card companies offer points because they make money elsewhere, perhaps from people who don't pay their bills on time and end up paying high interest rates. It's true that credit card companies make a significant amount from interest charges. In Australia, for example, around 20% to 25% of people don't pay their bills on time, but recent data shows 45% of credit card balances are accruing interest. However, when we examine the amount of money collected from these individuals, it's not enough to give away free points to the other 75% to 80% of people who do pay their bills on time and still make a profit with minimal risk. The actual cost lies in the fees that merchants pay to accept credit cards, which typically range from 1% to 2% of each transaction.

Many businesses build these fees into their prices, so they won't offer a discount if you use cash. However, some places provide cash discounts or allow you to pay for free using a debit card. You might instead pay an additional fee on your bill if you use a credit card. In Australia, a significant number of transactions offer supposedly 'free' points when you've actually paid around 1% for them. Using the example of someone with a $4000 monthly credit card bill, if only a quarter of those transactions had a 1% fee added, that's still an extra $25 per month paid for the privilege of using that credit card and earning points.

There are exceptions, though, including people who put their business expenses on a credit card and manage to earn points without paying extra fees. However, for the average person with a $4000 credit card bill, most cards offer one point per dollar spent, resulting in 4000 points a month or 48,000 points a year. While decades ago a one-way ticket to London might have cost around 50,000 points, everything has become more expensive – even in terms of points. In 2023, 48,000 points was enough for two return tickets from Sydney to Brisbane, typically costing around $400. To earn these 'free' tickets, you'd have to spend $48,000 on your credit card, averaging out to a monthly saving of around $33.

Ask yourself this question: what is the likelihood of staying within $33 of your monthly budget if every purchase is made with a credit card, compared with using your own bank account? Suppose you set a monthly spending limit of $3950, enforced by the Fast and Slow System bank account structure. If you go from spending $4000 a month on a credit card to $3950 using your own funds, that's a $50 monthly saving, amounting to $600 by the end of the year – enough to buy those two tickets to Brisbane with a couple of hundred dollars left over.

Looking at a range of studies on credit card spending, I couldn't find evidence of lower difference or no difference in spending when using a credit card. The lowest overspend across the studies was a 12% to 18% higher spend when using credit card compared to using cash. In our example, that 12% equates to $480 a month. So, the average person would have $480 in additional savings by not spending the money that their credit card would encourage them to spend, but they'd lose $33 a month by not getting the points. You would have to be not just different from the average but significantly different – within the lowest 0.5% of spenders – to get the $33 advantage of using points. For Rob and Claire, the difference was over $20,000 a year in additional savings, showing the more you earn, the more you stand to lose by using a credit card.

A short-term compromise for those of you who can't part with your credit cards and points is to remove the credit card from your wallet and unlink it from your phone and watch. You can still have your bills go through the credit card, earning points from necessary expenses while keeping discretionary spending separate. Of course, this will reduce the number of points you earn, but it significantly increases the likelihood of achieving the financial goals you set out to reach.

In conclusion, the allure of rewards points can often overshadow the hidden costs and potential overspending associated with credit card usage. By taking a step back and evaluating your spending habits, you can determine whether the points you could earn are genuinely worth the potential drawbacks. For most people, using a debit card or strictly limiting credit card usage to necessary expenses can lead to greater savings and more effective budget management. Ultimately, the key is to find a balance that works for you and aligns with your financial goals.

Offset or savings accounts with a credit card – even worse!

The second logical argument for keeping a credit card is the belief that you can use the bank's money for free, which you can then put into a savings account or an offset account linked to your home loan, enabling you to pay off your mortgage more quickly or build your savings faster. Unfortunately, this myth is often promoted by banks and some finance professionals who assume that people spend the same amount with or without a credit card. As we've discussed, however, this assumption is often incorrect.

To keep things simple, let's assume a 6% interest rate on an offset account linked to a mortgage. In this case, we save 6% interest on every dollar in the offset account. System 1 thinking might tell us that we're saving money, but System 2 thinking needs to calculate the actual benefit, so let's use Jack's and Amy's choices as examples.

Jack has a $4000 monthly credit card bill, while Amy chooses to use her own money. At the end of the month, Jack has the $4000 he would have spent now sitting in his offset account, while Amy has already spent her money. If Jack keeps doing this for the whole year, the one-time $4000 benefit will be sitting against his offset account, saving him 6% interest. So, how much does Jack save?

Table 10.1: Jack's monthly spending using an offset account

Target spend/month	$4000
Interest saving/month	$20
Net theoretical spend/month	**$3980**

As shown in table 10.1, over the course of the year, Jack saves 6% of $4000: $240, which is only $20 a month. In other words, if Amy sets a budget of $3980, just $20 a month less than Jack, she'll finish the year level with Jack in terms of savings.

The probability of Amy saving $20 a month by using her own money is significantly greater than that of Jack managing to stay within $20 of his $4000 budget. Jack only has to spend $5 more a week and he'll be worse off than if he didn't have the credit card. Meanwhile, if Amy cuts her monthly expenditure down to $3800 a month (just 5% less than Jack's $4000), by the end of the year she'll have saved $2400, whereas Jack will still only have saved $240 by using a credit card linked to his offset.

If Amy tries to stick to the $3800 budget using only her pay account, she'll have not much more chance of sticking to it than Jack. However, if she puts $350 a week into her weekly spending account, $1000 a month into her fun account and $500 a month into her holiday savings account, and allows $780 a month for bills, she will most likely stick to that budget. That will give her a $6000 holiday for the year (in comparison to Jack's 48,000 credit card points), or she'll have saved way more than Jack, see table 10.2.

Table 10.2: Amy's monthly spending using the Fast and Slow System

Bills account/month	$780
Weekly spend for average month	$1520
Fun account/month	$1000
Holiday savings/month	$500
Actual spend/month	**$3800**

If you're still not convinced at this stage, there are only one or two possible explanations. First, you're an extreme tight-arse who loathes spending money, in which case you won't be spending $4000 a month. Second, your System 1 thinking may have tricked your System 2 thinking once again, convincing you that the credit card addiction isn't causing you any harm. Either way, you'll never know for sure if you don't try it for yourself; try letting all your bills (except for groceries) continue going through the card, but leave the card at home and try the weekly/monthly spending plan. Monitor your spending for three months and, if it's identical to when you used the credit card, with no benefit for you, then by all means go back to it and tag or message me on social media to tell me I was wrong.

Summary

- Using a credit card for all spending will keep you spending fast, but they are addictive and habits are hard to break.
- Buying things and the pain of paying are decoupled by credit card use, leading to higher overall spending.
- People who have stopped using their credit cards have succeeded in hitting their savings goals or paying off their mortgage faster than those who haven't.
- The benefit of points doesn't outweigh the cost of using credit cards.
- Using the bank's money for 'free' typically saves users less than the annual credit card fee, and any interest earned or saved is extremely unlikely to offset the savings to be made from sticking to a spending plan.

PART III

EXECUTION IS EVERYTHING

Chapter 11

Implementation and accountability

The aim of this book is to help people find a better way to manage their money, take control of their spending, reach their goals and ultimately live a happier and more fulfilled life. However, like all common-sense and good ideas, everything falls over if the implementation isn't right.

In an ideal world, you'd rearrange your bank accounts, set up new accounts and establish automatic payments in a way that encourages you to save more for tomorrow while simultaneously setting money aside for your different goals. However, many people try to find an easier solution that's close enough to the principles without making every change. This is because changing where you bank or using a new debit card can feel difficult, awkward or uncomfortable. Keeping all your savings in one place and tracking them with a spreadsheet might seem like a simpler alternative to setting up different savings accounts. Of course, we know from chapter 6 that these compromises are likely to lead to worse outcomes.

In this chapter, we'll address the big questions related to managing bank accounts. What should you do with your current bank accounts? Should you keep them or open new accounts? How should you choose a new bank? What about fees? How do you stay on track? What should you do now?

We'll examine various examples of how people have changed their habits and behaviours, moving forward with their knowledge of the Fast and Slow System. By addressing these questions and looking at real-life examples, you'll be better equipped to implement the strategies and advice to ultimately lead a more financially stable and fulfilling life.

What should you do with your current bank?

It's fascinating how loyal we can be to our bank, even when we know that they haven't done us any favours. They're just trying to sell loans and make money. If you opened your first bank account as a child, and the first $5 in that account were given to you by that bank, it can be hard to change. Many of us also feel stuck with our current bank due to the inertia caused by existing direct debits, passwords and mobile apps. There's also the issue of fees: many banks in Australia only offer fee-free banking if you deposit a minimum amount each month. However, there are dozens of other banks that offer fee-free banking without requiring a salary deposit. This is just System 1 thinking looking for excuses to be lazy so that we don't have to engage our System 2 thinking and solve the problem for our long-term financial goals.

The simplest solution, requiring the least amount of effort, is to continue to let your pay go into and direct debits come out of your current bank account. However, if you're not a tight-arse, it's essential to remove card access to this account from your wallet, phone and watch, as this will be your bills account. Disconnecting the phone banking app is also wise so you can't easily check balances or transfer money out. Keeping your current bank account is less likely to work if there's not a saver or a tight-arse in the household.

If you keep your current bank account for bills, you can set up a new bank account with a new bank or non-banking financial institution to use for all your spending within minutes. Fortunately, many banks make it easy to open new accounts online. Some even issue a digital card that you can download onto your phone or watch and use right away. This is what you want from your spending account, *not* your bills account, which is where your pay goes. You'll need a transaction account and a savings account with the new bank. These will be your weekly spending and 'fun' accounts, respectively. As I've mentioned before, it's a good idea for couples to have separate accounts for individual spending. This way, each person can manage their spending without affecting the other.

To implement this, set up automatic payments from your bills account to deposit weekly amounts into your weekly transaction accounts and monthly amounts into your 'fun' account, plus regular deposits on payday to your other savings accounts (for your future and shorter-term goals, such as holidays). Figure 11.1 (overleaf) is an illustration of this set-up.

The Golden Eggs web app helps you work out how much should be transferred automatically into each account each week, month and pay cycle (this can be viewed in the summary PDF via the print icon). Otherwise, simply set up the weekly and monthly transfers to the fun account, taking care to make sure the weekly transfer happens on a day when groceries can be bought before anything else. The other savings can be transferred in line with pay cycles, usually the higher income earner's.

Figure 11.1: Sample banking set-up using the Fast and Slow System

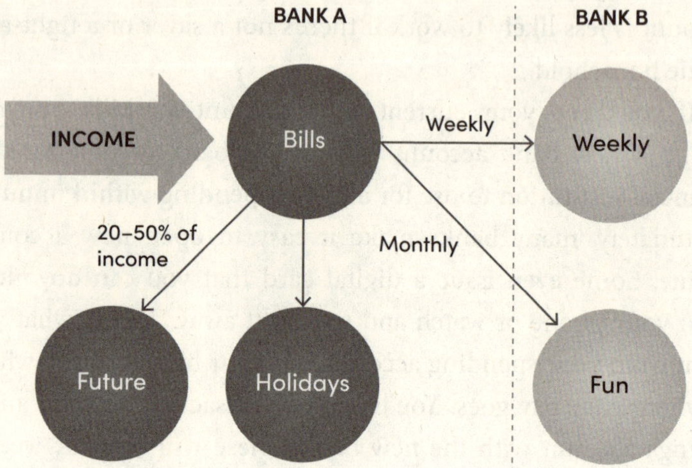

How to pick a new bank

Setting up with a new bank can feel quite daunting at first. This is especially true if you've recently set up a whole new collection of bank accounts following advice from outside of this book. But, if your direct debits for bills have been set up, that could now be your bills account, and that bank will be known as your 'old' bank. Now you need a new bank to separate out discretionary spending from bills and savings. If you are single and a spender or shopaholic, or in a couple where both are spenders or shopaholics, then consider using your old bank as your spending bank and use a cash management account (more on that in a moment) for your pay and bills.

The key is to deliberately make it inconvenient to move funds from Bank A to Bank B. This will stop our System 1 thinking from having too much control. When we want something and don't have enough money in our account, we don't want our System 1 thinking to instantly transfer funds to our new spending bank. We don't want a low, high or drunk version of ourselves to take over in a weak moment. If it takes a day to move money, we give ourselves a chance to engage System 2 thinking.

When looking for a new bank, use the following pointers to help you make your decision:

- Try to avoid instant-transfer capabilities. Most banks in Australia now allow instant transfers between institutions, making it too easy to transfer between banks. Some credit unions may still take time for transfers. Eventually we'll have the option to set time delays on transfers, but none offer this deliberate inconvenience at the time of writing.
- If your new bank will be for bills and savings, consider a cash management account (CMA). CMAs are offered by some banks outside of the instant-payment system, as they're designed for investing and self-managed super funds, but they can be great for saving and bill payments because they have no card access but pay interest on credit balances. Kelly and I use Macquarie Bank. It has regular accounts connected to cards, but their CMA takes a day to move funds to our spending accounts and we can still BPAY and automatically transfer to other accounts, so it's great for our bills.
- Make sure the accounts are fee free, as you're going to need quite a few. More and more of these fee-free accounts are appearing, especially through neobanks. Some neobanks claim to help with budgeting through categorisation and alerts, but like spend-tracking apps they don't physically stop us spending when we shouldn't; they merely point out our deficiencies for us to beat ourselves up about with later.
- If everything can happen in an instant, then try unlinking the bills bank app from your phone and hiding the passwords

from yourself. That way, if you want to move money instantly, you'll need to re-download the app and remember your login details before moving the money. It's still possible, but maybe only when you're sober and rational!

If you feel the need to temporarily spend over budget due to shared expenses with others (on a group holida or when putting on aa celebration, for example), please don't take from savings or bills and then take cash back from the group, which you know will only get spent. Great apps like Beem It, Splitwise and Venmo exist to help with bill-splitting and shared expenses for holidays and other special events, but it's always better to pick an amount you're all happy to put into a kitty.

What about emergencies?

What if you get rid of credit cards so only have access to limited funds in spending accounts, and there's an emergency? This is a normal fear, but psychological research suggests we overestimate the occurrence of bad things. Let's assume first that the threat is real. The obvious solution that you might jump to is keeping a credit card just in case. This is likely to be a slippery slope, as your System 1 thinking starts to classify mild inconveniences as worthy of using the credit card.

To understand better, let's look at some typical 'emergencies':

- Medical emergency – something bad has happened and you need to pay for unexpected expenses.
- Travel – you're travelling and suddenly stuck with a need to access funds or leave a hire car deposit, or an overseas family emergency has cropped up and you need to buy tickets today.
- Petrol – you've just filled up and found there's not enough money in the account to pay.

- Eating out – you've accidentally over-ordered or you're out with friends and your share of the bill is more than you have.
- Shopping – you've arrived at the checkout with more than you can afford to cover.

The first two sound like true emergencies, while the last three all seem to have the characteristics of bad planning. Checking our balance before filling up, ordering food or going shopping will solve most of these issues. Back in the days of cash, these were always problems you had to solve beforehand, so using them as an excuse to keep a credit card seems lazy.

Keeping an emergency credit or debit card in the car or having emergency cash are all ways of solving the first two problems. Importantly, if any of the last three problems occur, having a card in the car, not in our wallet or linked to our phone or watch, forces us to return to the car before completing the transaction, which normally triggers our System 2 thinking. If the emergency is just that we've arrived at the check-out over-budget, this usually results in us realising that it's not worth going back to the shops. It also acts as a form of punishment, or 'pain', for bad planning that we'll want to avoid in the future.

Imagine we're at the shops with a debit card linked to a spending account and there's only $20 left in that account. We don't check the balance before we get to the checkout, and we suddenly find that we've actually spent $35. It's a little bit embarrassing at the time and our System 1 thinking tells us that what we need to fetch the card from the car. However, as we head to the car, our System 2 has the opportunity to kick in and start rationalising whether pulling money out of the emergency card is really what we want to do. Maybe we could go back and cut the bill down to $20. The easiest thing to do, however, is to drive away. System 1 would at this point be telling us it's embarrassing to go back in, so let's just drive away and pretend it didn't happen. If it's a genuine emergency – for example, we need to buy some petrol because we're on a journey, or we have to pay a medical bill for treatment that we've already had – we'd go back.

When we use our own psychology against ourselves like this, we tend to be able to think first and stop ourselves from spending the extra money. The great thing is, when money is landing weekly, it'll only be a few days until more money arrives and we can do the things that we want to do again.

A debit card linked to a labelled 'emergency' account is normally the best option for these situations, especially if it's with the bank where we keep our savings and pay bills. We shouldn't need to borrow money from a bank through a credit card to cope with life's emergencies.

The only exception I have found to my general ban-all-credit-card stance relates to travel. I have found when travelling that several car hire companies won't take a debit card for the deposit. If that means you take a credit card with you when you travel once a year and treat it as something you only use for transport, then so be it. The risks of overspending, if this is all you use it for, are as close to zero as possible.

Many of us who grew up with cash keep a back-up $50 hidden in our phone case, key ring or wallet and try to forget it exists. We can use it in an emergency, knowing that the next time we get a chance we'll need to draw out cash and replenish it. I recently found a $20 note folded up inside a key ring and realised that I hadn't used that key ring for three or four years! Luckily the $20 note is still legal tender, so there's no issue.

Either way, if we've got our fun money in a savings account with the same bank as our everyday spending account, we can instantly access more funds in most emergencies. The spending bank is the bank we want to have linked to our phone apps and any online spending, so it acts as the first barrier to guard against emergencies while protecting our bills account and other savings.

Implementing the Fast and Slow System

What I will try to do now is give some examples of what has worked for my clients, demonstrating some adaptations that are suited to different people at different points in time.

Classic couple scenario: Mitch and Grace

In chapter 9 I introduced you to Mitch and Grace and their tendencies to underestimate what they were spending and to overspend relative to their income – not surprising, since it turned out they were both spenders. The great thing is they were model students from day one. They just wanted to listen, learn and make whatever changes were necessary to change their habits and get better with money. With their permission, I've shared their goals as they set them out when we met at the start of the process in table 11.1 (overleaf).

It took just two weeks to set up their new banking structure (figure 11.2, overleaf) using the Fast and Slow System, and within three months all their habits had completely changed. Suddenly money made sense to them. They knew the money in the spending accounts was OK to spend and it didn't matter what they spent it on. When I asked if they were dipping into savings, the answer was a resounding 'No'.

One of their most important items of expenditure was tithing, or charitable giving, through their church. They continue to do this in addition to hitting their other savings goals and adding to a Christmas savings account throughout the year.

Table 11.1: Mitch and Grace's goals

Goal area	1–2 years	3–10 years	11–30 years
Relationship/ family/schooling	• Start family (2020)	• 2–4 kids total • Church primary school (from 2026)	• Church high school (from 2033)
Where and what to live in	• Continue renting from parents	• Consider renting bigger place	• Buy a five-bedroom forever home (by 2033)
Investments	• Buy first investment property (and maybe a second)	• Use trusts to keep buying (minimum three)	• Generate passive income to cover expenses
Career	• Mitch to upgrade to senior role • Grace to take parental leave	• Mitch to maintain senior position • Grace to work part time	• Mitch to retire by 45 to volunteer more • Grace to retire by 40 to volunteer more
Holidays	• Local holidays each year	• Alternate local with overseas holidays every two years	• Travel more often for longer
Celebrations, cars and other big things	• Mitch's 30th (2020) • First wedding anniversary (2021)	• Grace's 30th (2027) • Kids' 10th birthdays (from 2029) • Upgrade to a seven-seater vehicle	• Mitch's and Grace's 40ths (2030, 2037) • Kids 18ths (from 2038)

Figure 11.2: Mitch and Grace's banking structure

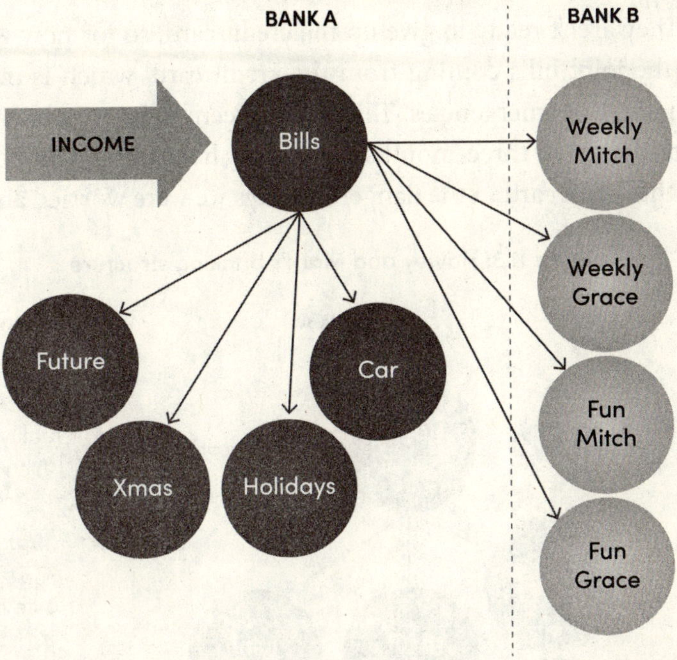

Separate and together: Hayley and Mark

Mitch and Grace's situation is a classic couple scenario, but that set-up isn't going to suit everyone, of course. Hayley and Mark, for instance, are not married and want to keep an element of their finances separate. This is what we worked out for them.

As illustrated in figure 11.3 (overleaf), both Hayley and Mark have a separate bills account where their pay lands, plus a joint bills account where most of the bills are paid from. Individual bill accounts are for things such as gym memberships and phone bills, while rent, electricity, internet and insurances are shared bills that come out of their shared account. Hayley's and Mark's future accounts are also kept separate, but they merged their holiday account because they aren't planning to go on holiday without one another.

They aren't ready to give up the credit card, so for now we've left the joint bills coming from the credit card, which is in the car in case of emergencies. This doesn't seem to be a problem for them, as at their three-months review they hadn't been tempted to use the credit card in the dangerous ways we were worried about.

Figure 11.3: Hayley and Mark's banking structure

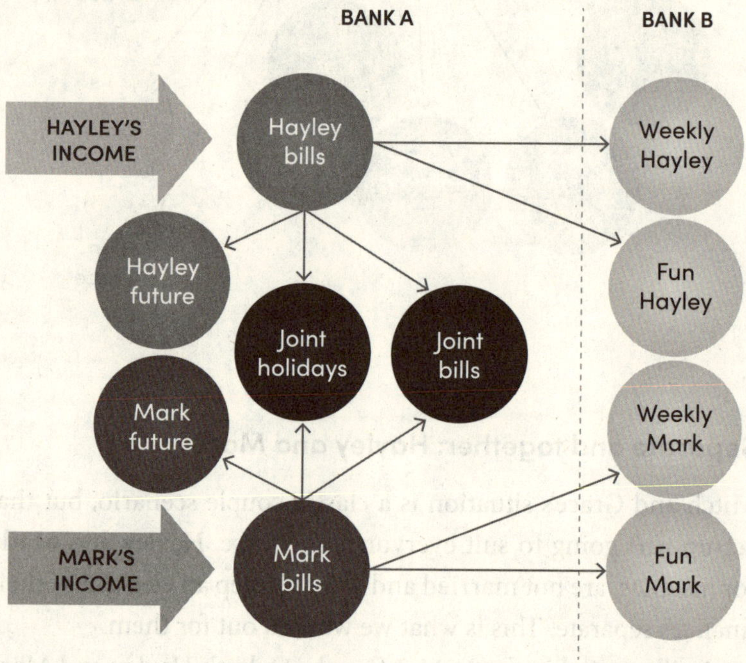

Though it might look complex, everything is automated, and both Hayley and Mark see only their own four accounts and two joint accounts. They still live most of their lives from their two spending accounts, just like everyone else using the Fast and Slow System.

How do you stay on track?

As described by James Clear in *Atomic Habits*, accountability is an essential component of making positive changes in our lives. Instead of relying solely on motivation, Clear suggests focusing on the beginning of any new habit, making the changes necessary to start it and incorporating accountability.

Clear stresses the importance of making a statement of intent, linking our intention with a specific place and time. This method helps to trigger our memory and ensure we follow through with our plan. For example, I struggled to make progress on writing the final chapters of this book. Following Clear's advice, I committed to going outside into the courtyard immediately after lunch and starting my writing there. This meant that during lunch I was already thinking about writing. Likewise, the location was important. If I'd just planned to write after lunch, I might have gone back into my office with my laptop, phone and paperwork and become distracted. Going outside after lunch meant I had nothing else to do but sit in a very sunny courtyard, with a rather delicious cup of coffee, and start dictating the next section.

There are three main approaches to implementing the Fast and Slow System. You can do it all yourself, do it with someone else or have someone else to do it for you. Each approach is built on a different accountability structure, so I'll run through all three now to help you decide which is right for you.

Do it yourself

Make your own statement of intent, not just a vague plan to do it on the weekend. Be more specific and set up a trigger. For example: 'When we get home from work tonight, we'll get on the laptop, calculate a budget and open up new bank accounts to help us start the process of changing how we manage money.'

Then you could simply put your laptop down near where you would normally sit. Then, instead of sitting down in front of the TV as you might usually, you can pick up your laptop and move to the dining table. If you use a wall calendar, you could circle the date when you're going to take the next step. If you miss ticking it off, you'll have to keep rescheduling, which might be irritating enough to make you get the job done.

Do it with someone else

Doing it with someone else means it's still down to you to act, but you have tools to guide you and friends to hold you accountable. To make the process more enjoyable and motivating, you can use the Golden Eggs web app. This tool provides a 'do it with me' experience, with lots of videos to guide you through the goal setting process, setting up your new bank account structure and implementing automations. If you and a friend plan to do it together, you can periodically check in with each other at a specific time and place. For example, you might meet for a coffee on the first Sunday of every month to ensure everything is running smoothly and adjust if necessary. This shared accountability helps keep you both on track, while the structured approach will ensure you don't skip steps or get the maths wrong.

Have someone else do it for you

If you need additional support, you can pay someone to help you. The Golden Eggs web app provides the option to hire a personal money coach to assist you on your journey. The app will automatically suggest this for spender and shopaholic singles and couples. This service is separate from the app and designed for those who prefer a more hands-on and supported approach to working out their figures and setting up automations. You can schedule a call with your money coach at a specific time and place, such as at your home office on a weekday evening, to work together on organising your finances. The aim of this coaching is to set you up for long-term success, so within a few months you'll be happily managing on your own. If you're already in real strife, you could also try mybudget.com.au, which takes over all management of bills and transfers for you but requires the payment of ongoing fees.

By incorporating accountability into your new financial habits, you increase the likelihood of success. Each of these approaches has advantages and drawbacks, so choose the one that best suits your needs and preferences, especially taking into account your money personality. Whether you decide to manage your finances on your own, with the assistance of an app or with the guidance of a personal money coach, setting a specific time, place and prompt for each task will help you stay on track and achieve your financial goals.

What do you need to do now?

Now that you understand the importance of accountability and have chosen an approach that works best for you, it's time to start implementing your new financial habits. Here are the steps to follow:

1. **Assess your current financial situation.** Use your own spreadsheet, an online tool or the Golden Eggs web app to enter and categorise all your expenses, including bills, insurance and other periodic payments. The Golden Eggs app can import and categorise expenses from your bank accounts, or you may be able to find and use another app with a similar function.

2. **Analyse your discretionary spending.** Determine how much you're currently spending on non-essential items and services, but don't dwell on past spending habits. Instead, focus on setting a realistic budget for discretionary expenses moving forward.
3. **Set financial goals.** Establish specific objectives, such as saving for a trip to Europe in five years. Calculate how much you'll need to save annually to achieve your goals and include these figures in your budget.
4. **Open new bank accounts with a different bank.** To ensure you are banking with at least two separate institutions, open new accounts with a different bank to your primary bank.
5. **Inform your payroll department.** Notify your payroll department about any changes to which account you'd like your salary deposited to so your income is directed to the correct account.
6. **Automate your finances.** Create a list of automatic transfers to be made on a weekly, monthly or fortnightly basis. You can do this either manually or using the Golden Eggs app. Then, set up these transfers online to ensure your money moves seamlessly between accounts without any manual intervention.
7. **Unlink old accounts and cards.** Remove any old banking apps, cards and account information from your phone and wallet if that bank is being used for bills. Keep these items securely at home to avoid any temptation to revert to your old habits.
8. **Begin your new financial journey.** Once everything is set up and your first payments have been made, start living according to your new financial plan.

9. **Review and stay accountable.** Regularly track your progress, review your spending and use one of the accountability approaches discussed earlier to stay on track with your financial goals.

By following these steps, you'll establish a solid foundation for your new financial habits and be well on your way to achieving your goals. Remember, success comes from consistency and commitment, so make sure you stay accountable and keep working towards a better financial future.

Rate your spending

One of the best exercises you can do is to keep track of not just what you spend your money on but how you spend it and how you feel about your spending. For the first few weeks of implementing the Fast and Slow System, I recommend keeping a journal or diary, or simply making some notes for yourself. If you have a partner, have a conversation each week about whether it was a good week, in which you felt pretty good about yourself and enjoyed your spending, or if you had a bit of a blowout and ran out of money too soon. If it was a problem for you, have the discussion, write down some notes and then resolve to do things differently and better the following week.

Most people find when they start out that their money runs out faster than they thought it would. A simple review should help them figure out why: for example, there wasn't enough money for the groceries because they had takeaway twice at the beginning of the week, they had a big night out, or the money landed on a Monday and they didn't go grocery shopping until the weekend. If there was a problem, have the discussion, write down notes and then resolve to do things differently and better next week – for example, perhaps weekly money should land *just* before grocery shopping.

Remember, it's better to make changes along the way than to give up on a system that works consistently for most people over very long periods of time. It's also important to note down when you might have been a bit disappointed, either in yourself or in the way that you spend money. Maybe you felt you missed out on something. Make those notes so you remember to prioritise things differently next time.

No matter how you review your week, I strongly recommend that you carry around two lists from now on. The first list should include life's simple pleasures – the things that make you feel good without costing much or any money. For example, a walk in the park, a trip to the beach, dinner with family, a phone call with an old friend or some exercise. The aim is to feel good about yourself so your System 1 thinking doesn't start looking for retail therapy.

As we get older, we realise that helping others makes us feel good. It could be as simple as helping a friend move house. Though you mean it when you offer, often friends won't ask for help because they don't want to put you out. If you can persevere and show up, hanging out with them and doing that helpful task will make you feel good while also making them feel valued and loved. As a society, if we had a lot more people helping lots more people, then lots more people would feel happy and loved.

The second list is Kelly's idea: a 'to-buy' list of items you're considering purchasing. This helps you to prioritise spending and make more informed decisions. Studies show that the anticipation of the item is as exciting as buying the item itself. We also know there's only a certain amount of money available and we need to make choices. The list helps when the month's fun money lands and we're wondering what to spend it on. It's much better to evaluate options in a list than just spend on the first thing we think of. As I've mentioned before, Kelly also finds that some things end up getting pushed off the list and never purchased, which is way better than wasting the money and then having them end up in landfill.

For example, we might put a new smartphone on the list, but then a few days later we might add a new outfit or a meal at a fancy restaurant with amazing reviews. Now we can look at them side by side and prioritise. In the absence of a list, we're quite likely to try to act on every impulse and run out of money before doing something we know we would've loved. Then we'll beat ourselves up about missing out or wasting money because we changed our mind. This list helps us avoid being sucked into impulse buying by advertising and promotions while also giving us a reason to ignore more advertising for something we've added to the list. It calms our System 1 impulses.

My wife and I have been running this system for a long time now and Kelly, a former shopaholic, has become an expert in making lists and researching how to get the best things at the best prices rather than buying on the first impulse. A couple of years ago, she saw an item at 40% off in the sales. She resisted the temptation to buy it and, instead, put it on the list. The price went back up and, though she couldn't bring herself to pay full price, she kept it on the list. A few months later it was back on sale again, and she reasoned that it was important enough to buy since it had stayed on the list – and she still got it on sale. This is an important lesson about the lure of sales: if it's promoted once, it'll probably be promoted again, so there's no need to get sucked in the first time.

Summary

- Unless we implement change and take responsibility for the outcome, nothing changes and we will continue to spend fast.
- To make the transition easier, keep your current bank accounts and use automated payments to the new accounts, but remove all instant access from wallets, phones and watches.
- Choose a new bank, ideally one that is slow to transfer funds to and from, and set up weekly and fun accounts.
- Have a plan for emergencies, such as a debit or credit card in the car.
- Delegate roles within a couple and plan regular review discussions until it feels normal and right.
- Set a specific time to set up the new structures and automate everything.
- Set up and maintain two lists: one for life's simple pleasures, or cheap fun, and a 'to-buy' list to help you prioritise, delay gratification and make better choices.

Chapter 12
Helping others

Helping others is a natural human tendency. As social animals, we want to contribute to the wellbeing of our community, and there are usually rewards for doing so – be that the good feelings we get from assisting an elderly person to cross the road or payment for performing a helpful task.

I'm amazed at how many opportunities there are to help other people when you look and listen for them. For instance, it might be easy to walk past a homeless person without acknowledging them, yet taking the time to sit down and listen to their story, perhaps buying them a sandwich or some groceries, can make a difference for both parties. Helping someone reach an item on a high shelf or assisting a stranger with a heavy object can also boost your mood and create a positive impact. I work in a building that is quite complicated and has poor signage, so people always get lost. I don't necessarily know where everything is, but if I see someone looking lost, it's not difficult to ask if they need help. If I walk together with someone to help find what they're looking for, that person feels a bit better about humanity, but it also makes me feel good. Interestingly, offers for help are almost always refused the first time, yet gratefully accepted the second time. We seem to want to be independent, yet we're grateful for having received the help.

In the context of money and managing finances, most people don't want to let other people know that they're having problems, even close friends and family. Money seems to be the last taboo topic. You're more likely to talk about your sex life or mental health than money. By contrast, it seems socially acceptable to talk about a problem solved. Sharing your own experiences of getting financially buff, overcoming financial challenges, implementing double banking or finding a helpful book (like this one) can open the conversation and encourage others to seek help or try new strategies.

Recommending resources that have helped you on your financial journey can benefit both you and the person you're sharing with. There are thousands of money books, many of which focus on what to invest in, including my own book about property investing: *Getting Your Money $hit Together*. This book *Spending, Fast and Slow*, is really the beginning of a long journey to becoming financially independent, and hopefully it will help you get more out of your life.

When helping others financially, it's important to consider whether you're truly helping or merely covering up a flawed system. Encouraging individuals to seek professional advice or make changes to their financial habits may be more beneficial than simply giving them money, for example. This is particularly important when it comes to supporting family members, especially children. It's crucial to teach people valuable life lessons instead of fostering a dependency on others.

In summary, helping others can be a rewarding experience for both parties. By being attentive to the needs of those around us, offering help, sharing our own experiences and providing guidance, we can make a positive impact on our community and grow together on our respective journeys towards financial independence.

Sharing the journey with friends

Encouraging friends to take control of their money feels awkward and taboo, but there are other ways of bringing them along on your financial journey. As I've already mentioned, sharing your story with friends might be a good place to start. Another interesting tactic to use is asking them for help.

Returning to the idea of accountability, which was discussed in chapter 11, think about how much easier it is to do something new or difficult with a friend than is it go it alone. For example, if you were thinking about exercising and you signed up for a local gym, then said to your friend, 'Hey, I've signed up for a local gym and I'd really love someone to keep me company and go with me', it's normal for friends to say they were thinking about doing something similar and agree to join in. I worked out most consistently when I used to run on Monday and Wednesday mornings with one friend, and on Tuesdays and Thursdays with another. Every time I thought about sleeping in, I'd think about my friend and make sure to show up for them. The funny thing is, they said the same thing. These sorts of arrangements make it easier for both parties to stay on track.

The same is true when it comes to money. Committing to a process together can help you hold each other accountable. If you start using the Golden Eggs web app to change the way you're doing your banking, telling a friend about it is just like telling them you're signing up to the gym. Why not make getting financially fit a social activity too? You can remind each other of things you might have missed or forgotten. You might be surprised by how many friends would love to do that, rather than feeling like they're on their own.

When we link things to our community, we feel we're part of something bigger. We all want to belong and feel part of a community. If you're already part of a group that's into investing, for example, adding day-to-day money management could be good. Introducing the concepts from this book can help you to add value to your existing communities.

Interestingly, admitting that we're not perfect is often enough for our friends to admit that they have concerns of their own. This book is not really for people with big financial problems. It's much more beneficial for people who simply aren't doing as well as they want to be doing. We all want to get more out of life, save more and pay off the mortgage faster – so that's likely to be the way to begin having these conversations.

How to coach others

It's been said that to teach is to learn twice. One of the best ways to be better with managing money and hold yourself accountable is to coach others or expect to coach others in the future, whether they're friends or family members – or, if you're already a finance professional, then coaching clients. Setting a good example for others can be a powerful motivating factor for sticking to your own plan.

When Kelly and I first started on this journey of managing our money in a better way, our starting point was needing to have four bank accounts: one for bills, one for everyday transactions, one for the future and one for saving to spend later. We were in the habit of being paid monthly, so we set all the budgets monthly. Although it worked for us initially, there were stressful times – for example, when there was a five-week month or when the monthly money ran short. We didn't notice it so much because the system was so much better than what we'd been doing in the past, which was putting everything on the credit card.

Once I started coaching other people – specifically, charging a fee for coaching other people – I started to get feedback that it was stressful towards the end of the pay cycle and wasn't quite working. To solve this, I started recommending moving the main grocery spend from fortnightly or monthly to weekly. Through trial and error, I found that having a weekly budget in addition to a monthly budget was way more successful for my clients. For a time, I experimented with letting people who are paid fortnightly stick to that timeframe, but it just wasn't working, so I changed everyone to the monthly/weekly split – except my wife and I.

Then, one lovely day, Kelly and I were at home in our apartment, which had magnificent views and the Sydney Harbour Bridge in the background. I looked out, thinking, *Wow, what a beautiful place that we live in; how lucky we are to be where we are and in this moment*. I decided I should break the news to my wife, Kelly, that I thought we should change from doing everything monthly to doing some of it weekly instead. Her reaction was immediately skepticism.

'I don't want to change it', she said. 'I like what we're doing. It's working. I understand the money. I understand how it works. I don't want to change.'

My tactic, and my recommendation when you're coaching anyone, is never to try to convince anyone to change something forever, because it feels like a big commitment. It's like asking someone to get married when you only just met them. It was much easier to ask Kelly to try it for the next couple of months. For the next couple of months, we would break the monthly budget up into weekly and monthly amounts, making sure they balanced out. If you understand the power of inertia and how lazy we are as human beings, you'll realise, of course, that we never changed back from that position. In fact, we didn't even get around to reviewing that position until about five months later. Finally, I asked Kelly, 'How is it working on the new weekly cycle?' She said that she found it did work much better. She was much less stressed about having too much month left at the end of the money.

The trick with coaching anyone – whether it be a partner, children (especially teenagers), clients or friends – is to follow the same process that I set out in this book. Nobody wants to change their behaviour. Nobody wants to change what they do and admit that what they've been doing isn't perfect, but everyone wants better long-term outcomes. This means we must always start with goals and current pain points.

People are motivated to change for one of two main reasons: to move towards something they believe is pleasurable (gain) or to move away from something they believe is painful (loss). Studies show people are more likely to take action to avoid pain than they are to move towards pleasure. The starting point, therefore, is asking these sorts of questions of your trainee to get them talking and engaged:

- How good do you think you are at saving?
- Do you ever get anxious about money or irritated about the amount of money that you're spending?
- Which would you choose between a $2000 holiday in Fiji or 50 $40 fast food vouchers?
- Are you saving up for a holiday as well as saving up for your future?

- Do you have card access to the account where your pay lands?
- Have you found that the more you earn, the more you spend?
- Based on your current rate of savings, how long is it going to take you to save up the deposit for your first home? How confident are you about that timeframe?

As I've mentioned before, the Golden Eggs team has built a web app, located at app.goldeneggs.info, to walk you through the process of setting up and managing a spending plan – everything from personality combinations to calculations on spending, paying down a mortgage and hitting savings goals. Plus, it can be integrated with your bank accounts to extract spending data before and after you set up a spending plan. It's accessible (with all the features) for the first month at no charge. One day it'll be a downloadable app, but as of 2023 it's fully online and best viewed via desktop rather than on a phone.

Teenagers

The group I would love to reach more quickly is teenagers aiming for their first jobs. If you're a teenager and have read this far, the next step should be obvious: start now. If you have teenagers you can influence in your life, think of where they are right now. They may be opening their first bank account to have their pay deposited in it and then expect to have a card linked to that account. If they can be convinced to open one bank account where pay lands and another bank account where they pay themselves pocket money, they will immediately be on the road to a better financial future.

The last thing we want to do with this group is tell them how much to spend and what to spend it on, but they'll certainly be motivated by the idea that their spending money is an amount that they choose to set as a weekly budget. If you think their weekly budget is too high, don't say anything. Let them try it. Whatever their weekly budget is, it's going to be tiny in comparison to the budget they might spend in the future or they might accidentally end up spending once they get their first full-time job after leaving school. It's far better that they learn their money mistakes with a little bit of money than when they have a lot more money. So, encourage them to set a weekly budget and review how it's gone in a couple of months' time. Remember: your opinion of how well it's going isn't particularly relevant. It's their opinion about how well they're going that counts. If they're annoyed at how much they're spending or how little they saved, then the only thing you can do is ask them whether they believe they set the right weekly budget.

Always be open to them learning for themselves and help them feel they can talk to you about money without being judged. They will judge themselves far more harshly than you ever could. The last thing you want is for them to resent you as imposing something on them. It's far better that they learn their own lessons that they'll stick to for life than just do what you say for a short period of time and then change their mind later when they suddenly hear about bright and shiny credit cards or how easy car and personal loan are to take out. They could get themselves into a whole heap of trouble from that point on. Even when it comes to things like credit cards and personal loans, all you can do is ask them to weigh up the pros and cons and recommend a trial. Negotiate how long they'll consider doing it for before they re-evaluate and have the opportunity to make a different decision.

The same goes for coaching friends, colleagues or clients. If we can't convince them to do things in the best way possible from day one, then we agree on a short-term compromise with a review period of no more than three months. Likewise, if there's a specific behaviour that we'd like them to try, then we only pitch it as a three-month trial. Nobody likes to change, but most of us are willing to try things that we think might help.

Wrap-up

One of the best ways of starting coaching someone is to give them a copy of this book. Encourage them to watch my videos on social media and YouTube to simplify some of the lessons.

Most important of all is to not shy away from talking about money. If no-one teaches us how to manage money when we're children, no-one helps us correct things when we're adults and no-one shows us a different or better way, then how can we be sure that what we're doing is any good? Is it worse or better than what everyone else is doing? The temptation is to think that everyone is doing better than us, which means that talking about money feels like admitting we're not very good at it. Yet we all feel like we ought to be good at managing money.

There are already lots of books explaining what to do with savings once you start. However, my aim with this book is to make saving not just predictable this month, or year, but also easier and easier to increase over time. This will mean you'll have more to invest, and be able to save for a home faster and pay it off way quicker. Plus, when you're ready to retire, you'll know how to make the money last and leave a greater legacy.

In the meantime, my only wish for you is that you set your own goals and put in place your plan for long-term happiness. Helping others is what brings me the most joy, and I hope you get to experience something similar.

Summary

- Helping others is a great way to increase your happiness without spending money.
- Talking about finance can feel taboo, but helping friends should be a motivating force to break the code of silence, especially if you ask them to help hold you accountable.
- Coaching others is a great way to embed learnings and hold yourself to a higher standard, but it does require much more questioning and listening than simply 'telling'. If this book has taken you on a journey and motivated you to change, then make sure you help others go on the journey for themselves.
- Teenagers are in the perfect position, ideally before they get their first pay slip, to avoid the mistakes we've all made.
- The more we talk about money and try to help others, the happier and wealthier we all will be.

Acknowledgements

Writing a book is a huge commitment in time and energy, none of which would be possible without the help and support from Kelly at home and the Golden Eggs team at work: Christian, Amy, Nirmal, Michael, Phoebe, Mary, Rezzy, Niki and Jewel. Christian Kearns has been brilliant at actively reducing my day-to-day workload to help me focus on the bigger picture, long-term stuff like writing.

Without the inspiration, tools and training from the team at Dent Global, I would never have written my first book, let alone followed the process again to write a second one.

Any final manuscript has to go through a selection of test readers, whose feedback has helped me to add more examples, tables and clarity, to improve the reading experience. Special thanks to Ian, Efim, Matt and Sharon, John Banks, Ciska and Chris, who all gave way more detailed feedback than I initially expected.

Many of the stories and examples in the book are from real people, most of whom allowed me to keep their names and add to the authenticity of the content. I am grateful to them all. For those who preferred to remain anonymous, I'm also thankful to have met you and learned from the shared experience.

Thanks to Lesley and the team from Major Street for their support in getting this into bookstores around the country and spreading the word. Special thanks to Lauren through the editing process for holding me to a higher standard to make this a much better book than my initial draft.

About the author

Max grew up in a family of nine kids, aiming not to be poor. At 21 he met Kelly, a natural shopaholic, and for the next 11 years found the more they earned, the more they spent. He graduated with a Bachelor of Economics with honours from Manchester University and had a successful career with a multinational, which took him to Bangkok and Ho Chi Minh City. He loved his two years as a maths teacher in the UK, but when the family moved to Australia he found his UK qualification wasn't recognised. To support the family until Max could return to teaching, he and Kelly started a mortgage broking business, then discovered that almost everyone needs a financial education, not just lessons in high school maths.

Now Max is a professional property investor, with 16 rentals, 14 years of experience in finance and qualifications in mortgage broking and financial planning. These days, he spends his time coaching people on money management, property investing and good long-term loan structuring. He wants others to learn from the mistakes he made to gain the same – or greater – success.

When he takes a break, it's to travel with the love of his life, Kelly, or to spend time with his grandson, Matthew.

Max and his businesses have taken the 1% pledge, so that 1% of all revenue is directed to improving education in developing countries.

You can find Max here:

- TikTok – @maxatgoldeneggs
- LinkedIn – au.linkedin.com/in/goldeneggsmaxphelps
- Facebook – facebook.com/goldeneggsmoney
- Website – goldeneggs.info
- Golden Eggs web app – app.goldeneggs.info

References

Introduction

Kahneman, D, *Thinking, Fast and Slow*, Farrar, Straus and Giroux, New York, 2011.

Peetz, J, 'The "budget fallacy": Sources of accuracy and bias in personal spending predictions', *Theses and Dissertations (Comprehensive)*, 1101, 2010, scholars.wlu.ca/etd/1101.

Chapter 1: A brief history of money and the elimination of friction

Collins, J, 'A short history of the debit card', *Marketplace*, 18 August 2011, marketplace.org/2011/08/18/short-history-debit-card.

Diners Club International, 'Diners club history', accessed 5 September 2023, dinersclub.com/about-us/history.

Evans, DS, & Schmalensee, R, *Paying with Plastic*, MIT Press, Cambridge, 2000.

Ferguson, N, *The Ascent of Money*, Penguin, London, 2008.

Giordano, C, 'Australian cricket journalist charged £55,000 for bottle of beer in Manchester', *Independent*, 5 September 2019, independent.co.uk/news/uk/home-news/beer-malmaison-manchester-australia-cricket-journalist-a9093526.html.

Services Australia, 'How much you can get', 20 March 2023, servicesaustralia.gov.au/how-much-age-pension-you-can-get?context=22526.

Soman, D, 'The effect of payment ransparency on consumption: Quasi-experiments from the field', *Marketing Letters*, vol. 14, no. 3, 2003, pp. 173–183.

Chapter 2: Money, happiness and decision-making

Andrews, CG, 'Anticipation is the happiest part of a travel journey', *Natural Habitat Adventures*, 2 October 2018, nathab.com/blog/anticipation-is-the-happiest-part-of-a-travel-journey/.

Baxter, J, & Warren, D, *Families in Australia Survey: Families' concerns about finances*, Australian Institute of Family Studies, November 2021, aifs.gov.au/research/research-reports/families-concerns-about-finances.

Cleveland Clinic, 'Why retail "therapy" makes you feel happier', *healthessentials*, 21 January 2021, health.clevelandclinic.org/retail-therapy-shopping-compulsion.

Dunn, E, & Norton, M, *Happy Money: The new science of smarter spending*, Oneworld Publications, London, 2023.

The Giving Pledge, 'About the Giving Pledge', accessed 5 September 2023, givingpledge.org/about.

Helliwell, JF, Huang, H, Wang, S, & Norton, M, 'Chapter 2: Happiness, Benevolence, and Trust During COVID-19 and Beyond', *World Happiness Report 2022*, World Happiness Report, 18 March 2022, worldhappiness.report/ed/2022/happiness-benevolence-and-trust-during-covid-19-and-beyond.

Kahneman, D, *Thinking, Fast and Slow*, Farrar, Straus and Giroux, New York, 2011.

Morewedge, CK, Holtzman, L, & Epley, N, 'Unfixed resources: Perceived costs, consumption, and the accessible account effect', *Journal of Consumer Research*, vol. 34, 2007, pp. 459–467.

Nawijn, J, Marchand, MA, Veenhoven, R, & Vingerhoets, AJ, 'Vacationers happier, but most not happier after a holiday', *Applied Research in Quality of Life*, vol. 5, no. 1, 2010, pp. 35–47.

Nelissen, R, 'Abundance Causes Greed in Appropriation from Common Resources', *Psychology and Developing Societies*, vol. 34, no. 1, 2022, pp. 25–44.

Nichols, M, 'Bill Gates charity man happy to help billionaires give', *Reuters*, 7 August 2010, reuters.com/article/us-wealth-philanthropy-gatesfoundation/bill-gates-charity-man-happy-to-help-billionaires-give-idUKTRE6753U020100806.

Nolan, T, 'Must-read marriage advice from husband & wife divorce lawyers', LinkedIn, 9 February 2021, linkedin.com/pulse/must-read-marriage-advice-from-husband-wife-divorce-lawyers-nolan.

Scott, SB, Rhoades, GK, Stanley, SM, Allen, ES, & Markman, HJ, 'Reasons for divorce and recollections of premarital intervention: Implications for improving relationship education', *Couple and Family Psychology*, vol. 2, no. 2, 2013, pp. 131–145.

TheGlobalEconomy.com, 'Australia: Happiness index', accessed 5 September 2023, theglobaleconomy.com/Australia/happiness.

Van Boven, L, & Gilovich, T, 'To do or to have? That is the question', *Journal of Personality and Social Psychology*, vol. 85, no. 6, 2003, pp. 1193–1202.

Waldinger, R, & Liebergall, M, 'Author Talks: The world's longest study of adult development finds the key to happy living', McKinsey & Company, 16 February 2023, mckinsey.com/featured-insights/mckinsey-on-books/author-talks-the-worlds-longest-study-of-adult-development-finds-the-key-to-happy-living.

Weinschenk, S, 'Shopping, dopamine, and anticipation: What monkeys have to teach us about shopping', *Psychology Today*, 22 October 2015, psychologytoday.com/us/blog/brain-wise/201510/shopping-dopamine-and-anticipation.

Xu, AJ, Schwarz, N, & Wyer, RS-Jr, 'Hunger promotes acquisition of nonfood objects', *PNAS*, vol. 112, no. 9, 2015, pp. 2688–2692.

Zaltman, G, *How Customers Think: Essential Insights into the Mind of the Markets*, Harvard Business School Press, Boston, 2003.

Chapter 3: Understanding money

AAP, 'Benefits of multivitamins questioned', *SBSNews*, 14 February 2017, sbs.com.au/news/article/benefits-of-multivitamins-questioned/e5f9cz8f8.

Australasian Gaming Council, 'Economic contribution', accessed 8 September 2023, austgamingcouncil.org.au/fact-centre/economic-contribution.

Australian Bureau of Statistics, 'Australian national accounts: National income, expenditure and product', 6 June 2023, abs.gov.au/statistics/economy/national-accounts/australian-national-accounts-national-income-expenditure-and-product/latest-release.

id., 'Household expenditure survey,
Australia: Summary of results', 13 September 2023, abs.gov.au/statistics/economy/finance/household-expenditure-survey-australia-summary-results/2015-16.

Castles, I, *Information paper, 1975–76 household expenditure survey, Australia: Unit record file*, Australian Bureau of Statistics, 1994, abs.gov.au/websitedbs/D3310114.nsf/0/befd782091d98b54ca257203001fc2c2/$FILE/ATTQV9SE/1975-76%20%20Household%20Expenditure%20Survey%20CURF%20information%20paper.pdf.

Clean Up, 'E waste', accessed 5 September 2023, cleanup.org.au/e-waste.

id., 'Fast fashion', accessed 5 September 2023, cleanup.org.au/fastfashion.

id., 'How will you step up?', accessed 5 September 2023, cleanup.org.au/the-issues.

De La Rosa, W, & Tully, SM, 'The impact of payment frequency on consumer spending and subjective wealth perceptions', *Journal of Consumer Research*, vol. 48, no. 6, 2022, pp. 991–1009.

Melbourne Institute, 'Social indicator reports', accessed 5 September 2023, melbourneinstitute.unimelb.edu.au/publications/social-indicator-reports.

Milliman, RE, 'Using background music to affect the behavior of supermarket shoppers', Journal of Marketing, vol. 46, no. 3, 1982, pp. 86–91.

Morewedge, CK, Holtzman, L, & Epley, N, 'Unfixed resources: Perceived costs, consumption, and the accessible account effect', *Journal of Consumer Research*, vol. 34, 2007, pp. 459–467.

Thaler, RH, 'Mental accounting matters', *Journal of Behavioral Decision Making*, vol. 12, 1999, pp. 183–206.

Chapter 4: Goal setting

Australian Bureau of Statistics, 'Australian national accounts: National income, expenditure and product', 6 June 2023, abs.gov.au/statistics/economy/national-accounts/australian-national-accounts-national-income-expenditure-and-product/latest-release.

id., 'Average weekly earnings, Australia', 17 August 2023, abs.gov.au/statistics/labour/earnings-and-working-conditions/average-weekly-earnings-australia/latest-release.

Berman, R, 'Having a sense of purpose may help you live longer, research shows', *Medical News Today*, 21 November 2022, medicalnewstoday.com/articles/longevity-having-a-purpose-may-help-you-live-longer-healthier.

Dunn, E, & Norton, M, *Happy Money: The new science of smarter spending*, Oneworld Publications, London, 2023.

Live to 100: Secrets of the Blue Zones, Netflix, 2023.

Matthews, G, 'Goals research summary', Dominican University of California, 2020, dominican.edu/sites/default/files/2020-02/gailmatthews-harvard-goals-researchsummary.pdf.

MoneySmart, 'ASFA retirement standard', accessed 5 September 2023, moneysmart.gov.au/glossary/asfa-retirement-standard.

Services Australia, 'How much you can get', 20 March 2023, servicesaustralia.gov.au/how-much-age-pension-you-can-get?context=22526.

Sinek, S, *Start with Why: How great leaders inspire everyone to take action*, Portfolio, New York, 2009.

Vermeeren, D, 'Why people fail to achieve their goals', Reliable Plant, accessed 5 September 2023, reliableplant.com/Read/8259/fail-achieve-goals.

Warren, E, & Tyagi, AW, *All Your Worth*, Simon & Schuster, New York, 2005.

Chapter 5: Where are you now?

MoneySmart, 'Compound interest calculator', accessed 5 September 2023, moneysmart.gov.au/budgeting/compound-interest-calculator.

Australian Institute of Health and Welfare, 'Older Australians: Income and finances', 28 June 2023, aihw.gov.au/reports/older-people/older-australians/contents/income-and-finances#.

Chapter 6: Having a budget versus sticking to it

Hely, S, 'Why 86% of Australians don't know their monthly expenses', *Money*, 21 February 2018, moneymag.com.au/86-australians-dont-know-expenses.

Mint, 'Survey: 65% of Americans have no idea how much they spent last month', *Intuit*, 29 May 2020, mint.intuit.com/blog/budgeting/spending-knowledge-survey.

ubank, 'Know Your Numbers research – key findings', 15 May 2021, ubank.com.au/newsroom/kyn-2021-research-key-findings.

Chapter 7: The Fast and Slow System

Adeney, P, 'The shockingly simple math behind early retirement', *Mr. Money Mustache*, 13 January 2012, mrmoneymustache.com/2012/01/13/the-shockingly-simple-math-behind-early-retirement.

Earth List, 'Pete Adeney (Mr. Money Mustache) – Full Talk at WDS 2016 [HD]', *YouTube*, 29 October 2018, youtu.be/8BDWih309wc?si=Pu26l8vrAjZEa8tB.

Kahneman, D, *Thinking, Fast and Slow*, Farrar, Straus and Giroux, New York, 2011.

Morewedge, CK, Holtzman, L, & Epley, N, 'Unfixed resources: Perceived costs, consumption, and the accessible account effect', *Journal of Consumer Research*, vol. 34, 2007, pp. 459–467.

Nelissen, R, 'Abundance causes greed in appropriation from common resources', *Psychology and Developing Societies*, vol. 34, no. 1, 2022, pp. 25–44.

Networthify, 'When can I retire?', accessed 6 September 2023, networthify.com/calculator/earlyretirement?income=70000&initialBalance=0&expenses=25200&annualPct=5&withdrawalRate=4.

Thaler, RH, 'Mental accounting matters', *Journal of Behavioral Decision Making*, vol. 12, 1999, pp. 183–206.

Chapter 8: Personalised design

Dunn, E, & Norton, M, *Happy Money: The new science of smarter spending*, Oneworld Publications, London, 2023.

Chapter 9: Making it all add up

Australian Taxation Office, 'The super guarantee rate is increasing', 16 June 2023, ato.gov.au/Business/Small-business-newsroom/Lodging-and-paying/The-super-guarantee-rate-is-increasing.

Benartzi, S, 'Save More Tomorrow', accessed 6 September 2023, www.shlomobenartzi.com/save-more-tomorrow.

Burns, S, 'Why I never buy a new car: Warren Buffett', *New Trader U*, 26 April 2023, newtraderu.com/?s=why+I+never+buy+a+new+car.

Clason, GS, *The Richest Man in Babylon*, Penguin, New York, 2002.

Cluey Learning, 'Private school fees in Sydney', accessed 6 September 2023, clueylearning.com.au/en/school-fees/sydney-private-school-fees.

Courtney Facts, 'Are private schools better than public schools?', *ABC*, abc.net.au/news/2023-01-20/are-private-schools-better-than-public-schools/101867070.

Ellis, L, 'Housing in the endemic phase', Reserve Bank of Australia, rba.gov.au/speeches/2022/pdf/sp-ag-2022-05-25.pdf.

Piccione, T, 'The cost of Australia's most expensive private schools in 2023', *Canberra Times*, 4 January 2023, canberratimes.com.au/story/8033415/which-is-australias-most-expensive-private-school-in-2023.

Qu, L, & Baxter, J, *Divorces in Australia*, Australian Institute of Family Studies, March 2023, aifs.gov.au/research/facts-and-figures/divorces-australia-2023.

Thaler, RH, & Sunstein, C, *Nudge: Improving decisions about health, wealth, and happiness*, Penguin, London, 2009.

Chapter 10: Credit card addiction

Ajzerle, S, Brimble, M, & Freudenberg, B, 'A (w)hole in the financial budget: Budgeting's influence on the effective use of credit card debt in Australia', *Financial Planning Research Journal*, vol. 1, no. 1, 2015, pp. 55–72.

Banker, S, Dunfield, D, Huang, A, & Prelec, D, 'Neural mechanisms of credit card spending', *Scientific Reports*, vol. 11, no. 4070, 2021.

Commonwealth of Australia, *Report: Interest rates and informed choice in the Australian credit card market*, Australian Parliament House, 16 December 2015, aph.gov.au/Parliamentary_Business/Committees/Senate/Economics/Credit_Card_Interest/Report.

Cooke, G, 'Australian credit card and debit card statistics', *Finder*, 10 July 2023, finder.com.au/credit-cards/credit-card-statistics.

Diners Club International, 'Diners club history', accessed 5 September 2023, dinersclub.com/about-us/history.

Doyle, M-A, *Consumer Credit Card Choice: Costs, benefits and behavioural biases*, Reserve Bank of Australia, October 2018, rba.gov.au/publications/rdp/2018/pdf/rdp2018-11.pdf.

Durkin, TA, 'Credit cards: Use and consumer attitudes, 1970–2000', *Federal Reserve Bulletin*, September 2000, federalreserve.gov/pubs/bulletin/2000/0900lead.pdf.

Morewedge, CK, Holtzman, L, & Epley, N, 'Unfixed resources: Perceived costs, consumption, and the accessible account effect', *Journal of Consumer Research*, vol. 34, 2007, pp. 459–467.

Organisation for Economic Co-operation and Development (OECD), 'Household savings forecast', *OECD Data*, February 2019, data.oecd.org/hha/household-savings-forecast.htm.

Prelec, D, & Loewenstein, G, 'The red and the black: Mental accounting of savings and debt', *Marketing Science*, vol.17, no. 1, 1998, pp. 4–28.

Prelec, D, & Simester, D, 'Always leave home without it: A further investigation of the credit-card effect on willingness to pay', *Marketing Letters*, vol. 12, no. 1, 2001, pp. 5–12.

Radic, D, 'Cash vs. credit card spending statistics for 2023', *Moneyzine*, 25 February 2023, moneyzine.com/personal-finance-resources/cash-vs-credit-card-spending-statistics.

Reserve Bank of Australia, *Review of Card Repayments Regulation: Issues Paper*, March 2015, rba.gov.au/payments-and-infrastructure/review-of-card-payments-regulation/developments-card-payments-mkt.html.

Sarofim, S, Chatterjee, P, &Rose, R, 'When store credit cards hurt retailers: The differential effect of paying credit card dues on consumers' purchasing behavior', *Journal of Business Research*, vol. 107, 2020, pp. 290–301.

Soman, D, 'Effects of payment mechanism on spending behavior: The role of rehearsal and immediacy of payments', *Journal of Consumer Research*, vol. 27, 2001, pp. 460–474.

Tejani, S, *Poverty Lines: Australia – March Quarter 2023*, Melbourne Institute, March 2023, melbourneinstitute.unimelb.edu.au/__data/assets/pdf_file/0003/4710153/Poverty-Lines-Australia-March-Quarter-2023.pdf.

The Decision Lab, 'Pain of paying', accessed 6 September 2023, thedecisionlab.com/reference-guide/psychology/pain-of-paying.

Thomas, M, Desai, KK, & Seenivasan, S, 'How credit card payments increase unhealthy food purchases: Visceral regulation of vices, *Journal of Consumer Research*, vol. 38, no. 1, 2011, pp. 126–139.

Chapter 11: Implementation and accountability

Lieder, F, Griffiths, TL, & Hsu, M, 'Overrepresentation of extreme events in decision making reflects rational use of cognitive resources', *Psychological Review*, vol. 125, no. 1, 2018, pp. 1–32.

Weinschenk, S, 'Shopping, dopamine, and anticipation: What monkeys have to teach us about shopping', *Psychology Today*, 22 October 2015, psychologytoday.com/us/blog/brain-wise/201510/shopping-dopamine-and-anticipation.

Chapter 12: Helping others

Barberis, NC, 'Thirty Years of Prospect Theory in Economics: A Review and Assessment', *Journal of Economic Perspectives*, vol. 27, no. 1, 2013, pp 173–196.

Rakow, T, Cheung, NY, & Restelli, C, 'Losing my loss aversion: The effects of current and past environment on the relative sensitivity to losses and gains', *Psychonomic Bulletin & Review*, vol. 27, 2020, pp. 1333–1340.